Here's to more
Chicken dinners!
P9-CAR-420

Treasury of Chicken Cookery

Over 300 Delicious Ways to Prepare Chicken

Jane Novak

TREASURY OF CHICKEN COOKERY

Harper & Row, Publishers

New York   Evanston   San Francisco   London

DEDICATED, with respect, to all those enlightened cooks who don't care *which* came first, as long as the chicken is the end result

 For information address Harper & Row, Publishers, Inc., 10 East 53rd Street, New York, N.Y. 10022. Published simultaneously in Canada by Fitzhenry & Whiteside Limited, Toronto.

FIRST EDITION

Designed by Dorothy Schmiderer

Drawing by C. E. C. Cating-Moran

Library of Congress Cataloging in Publication Data

Novak, Jane.
Treasury of chicken cookery.
1. Cookery (Chicken) I. Title.
TX749.N68 1974 641.6'6'5 74-1842
ISBN 0-06-013227-2

Contents

Introduction

Gentle reader–cum–kitchen activist, the title of this book must not mislead you into endowing me with a one-track mind.

Indeed, my tastes in food are now and ever have been catholic. In my film-making days I was known to put raw onion on embarrassing quantities of caviar. More recently the onion has enhanced hamburgers, enchiladas, and certain Oriental dishes. During sometime calories-be-damned phases, I have created with my own hands such gourmet fare as *jambon en croûte*, soufflé Sarah Bernhardt, and a heavenly beef Wellington.

Yes, beef is beautiful. But ah! the chicken!

This lowly fowl is at once so basic, so satisfying, and—most important with today's soaring meat prices—so inexpensive a source of vital protein and general goodness, I feel compelled to publicize its almost unbelievable and thrifty versatility.

Indeed, with this book at hand, I promise you will be able to feast on fowl for days without end, with no fear of groans of "No! Not *again*!" from your family.

JANE NOVAK

1 Helpful Hints

How to Cope with Fowl

IN PRAISE OF POULTRY— THE REAL "NATURAL" FOOD

Chicken abounds in all those things nutritionists and health-food gurus insist are *good* for us: calcium, phosphorus, iron, thiamine, riboflavin, and niacin. Furthermore, chicken—of all "meats"—is lowest in calories, lowest in unsaturated fat, and one of nature's best sources of protein!

HOW TO PICK (NOT PLUCK) A CHICKEN

Freshness is the byword! If your neighborhood doesn't boast a genuine, old-fashioned poultry market where you can really pick and choose (at several cents premium per pound!) follow these guidelines in the supermarket:

Be sure the bird is plump. Its skin should be moist and blemish-free, with a definite golden cast (the clue to rich flavor). The breastbone—if you can locate it under its various plastic wraps—should be resilient when gently pinched between thumb and forefinger. The "pope's nose" should guard a delectable little nugget of fat up near the backbone.

TYPES OF CHICKEN, AND HOW TO EXPLOIT THEM

Today's breeding miracles have produced that wonderfully satisfactory, all-around bird commonly labeled the *broiler-fryer,* whose weight ranges from 2 to 3 pounds. But just to keep the record straight, women have been selecting for years from the following:

Broiler	1½–2½ lbs.	All-purpose, with emphasis on broiling
Fryer	2–3 lbs.	All-purpose, with emphasis on frying
Roaster	3–5 lbs.	Roast, bake, fry, sauté, fricassee
Capon	4–7 lbs.	Roast, bake, fry, sauté, fricassee
Stewing chicken	Over 3 lbs.	Stew, fricassee
Over-the-hill hen or rooster	Over 3 lbs.	Stock, broth, soup, ground or diced meat

HOW TO COMPUTE A CHICKEN, SERVINGS WISE

½ breast—1 serving

Thigh with attached leg—1 serving

3-pound bird—4 servings or approximately 2½ cups diced, cooked meat

HOW TO STORE A CHICKEN

In the Refrigerator. Remove the market packaging. Find and remove the packet of giblets (and usually the neck) inside the body cavity. (The giblets will make the basis of a fine stock and/or gravy.) Many authorities insist you rinse the bird, drain, and dry on paper toweling. I just rub the chicken all over with a cut lemon. (It's simply a matter of personal preference.) Wrap the bird very loosely in plastic wrap, foil, or waxed paper and place in the coldest part of the refrigerator. It will keep nicely *up to but no longer than 3 days*. If the chicken is cooked, refrigerate it separately from its juices, gravy, and/or stuffing.

In the Freezer. Remove the giblets, as above, and secure bird in an airtight bag before placing in the freezer. A whole chicken will keep for 12 months when stored at 0°. Pieces, packaged and stored as above, will keep for 6 months.

HOW TO DEFROST FROZEN BIRDS

Allow a frozen bird to defrost in the refrigerator in the bag or wrapper in which it was frozen. This is a slow process —at least overnight—but it ensures the least loss of flavor. If you are in a rush, place the frozen bird under cold, running water, gently moving the legs and wings away from the body and removing the giblets as soon as possible. Again, rinse and dry the chicken. Or follow my cut lemon technique.

HOW TO BONE A CHICKEN

Don't try! Unless you were born with a silver scalpel in your hand, heed my advice and rely solely on your poultry man's expertise. If he's anything like *my* "bird man," he'll take pleasure in showing off his incredible skill with the boning knife.

HOW TO TRUSS A CHICKEN

After having impaled myself rather painfully several times while attempting the use of needle and thread, *à la française*, I discovered I could achieve a satisfactory "truss" by simply using two pieces of ordinary kitchen string—like so:

Tie the tips of the drumsticks together. Do not cut ends

of string, but form a loop, capture the tail in it, then tie securely and trim the string. Fold the wing tips behind the back and tie. Form another loop with this string, secure the neck skin, and tie tightly. If the bird is to be spitted on a rotisserie, another length of string will keep the fleshy parts of the drumsticks snug against the body of the bird.

TO DISJOINT A CHICKEN

Remove the wings at the shoulder joints and fold into triangles. Remove each leg and thigh as a unit, first pulling the leg away from the body until the joint is easily discernible. Separate the thigh and drumstick at the "knee" joint. Using poultry shears, remove breast by cutting below the two bottom ribs and then along the sides. Divide the breast in half by cutting along the breastbone toward the shoulder joints, then cutting through the breastbone at about a 60-degree angle. Snip through the small joint in the forward part of the breast, making two neat pieces of white meat. If you want to use the back in your recipe instead of saving it for the stock pot, cut across the back just behind the last rib, then score the joint in the center of the back and break the spine. This will give you 10 pieces of chicken.

HOW TO CARVE A CHICKEN

I have long held to the theory that disjointing and carving are virtually the same thing, except that one *carves* for an audience. Personally, I can do without this particular spotlight.

I suggest two solutions: (1) Cook your bird in pieces and eliminate the need for public surgery; (2) simply follow the rules for disjointing, above. However, if you are carving a very large capon or roaster and would like to create neat breast slices, after removing the wings make a deep cut into the breast meat close to the wing joint and right down to the bird's frame. Starting halfway up the breast, thinly slice the white meat down to the initial deep cut. The little fillets will slide neatly onto the serving platter.

SOME FINAL NOTES

1. All recipes involving a 3-pound chicken may reasonably be expected to serve 4 persons. Any variance will be so indicated at the end of the recipe.

2. Butter and margarine are, of course, interchangeable, depending upon your individual cholesterol tolerance.

3. In certain recipes I have found it necessary, for reasons of the taste of the final product, to specify one or another of the many brand-name items found on supermarket shelves. I have not been subsidized by the manufacturer of any of them.

4. Measurements are accurate—according to my own taste. The adventurous cook doesn't live who will not adjust amounts to please her own palate.

2 Appetizers

Finger Food for the Happy Hour

The following recipes will serve an unknown quantity of guests, depending upon their individual appetites and the number of different finger foods you serve.

CHICKEN-LOBSTER CANAPÉS

½ cup minced, cooked chicken breast
½ cup minced, boiled lobster tail
Bottled tartar sauce to bind

Blend the ingredients lightly and spread on thin wheat crackers or toast fingers.

CHICKEN SALAD ROLLS

10 slices very fresh, soft white bread
Melted butter
1 cup chicken salad of your choice (see pages 27–32)
Watercress
Paprika
Tiny sweet gherkins for garnish (optional)

Cut the crusts from the bread and roll out the slices with a rolling pin until thin. Spread each thinned slice with melted butter and a thin layer of chicken salad. Place a sprig of watercress at either side, extending just beyond the edge of the bread. Roll up each slice like a jelly roll and secure with a toothpick. Arrange in a single layer on a tray, cover with a slightly dampened cloth, and refrigerate until well chilled. Before serving, cut each roll in half, dust with paprika, and garnish with more watercress or tiny sweet gherkins. (*Makes 20 roll-ups*)

LIVER PÂTÉ I

1 dozen chicken livers
¼ cup (½ stick) softened butter
2 teaspoons minced chives
½ teaspoon garlic powder
1 teaspoon onion salt
Salt and freshly ground pepper to taste
¼ cup mayonnaise or sour cream
1 tablespoon brandy

Cook the chicken livers in a little of the butter just until they lose color, then put them, along with the rest of the butter and the remaining ingredients, into the container of an electric blender and whir until the mixture is smooth and creamy. Transfer to a decorative bowl, chill, and serve with a variety of crackers and Melba toast.

LIVER PÂTÉ II

1 pound chicken livers
¼ cup (½ stick) butter
3 hard-cooked eggs
2 medium onions, cut up
Salt and freshly ground pepper to taste
2 tablespoons sherry
2 tablespoons mayonnaise
Sliced, stuffed olives for garnish

Sauté the chicken livers in the butter just until they lose color, then put them through the finest blade of a meat grinder (or whir in a blender), along with the eggs, onion, salt, and pepper. Blend in the sherry and mayonnaise until smooth, then turn into a buttered mold and chill.

Unmold on an attractive serving plate, garnish with sliced, stuffed olives, and surround with cocktail-sized rye bread or pumpernickel.

LIVER PÂTÉ III

Traditionally, this old-world pâté should be chopped by hand, giving it a unique texture, completely different from the blender-made pâtés. Whether you chop, grind or blend it, though, the flavor is distinctive and delicious.

1 pound chicken livers
2 tablespoons chicken fat or butter
1 small onion
2 hard-cooked eggs
3 to 4 sprigs fresh parsley
¼ cup light cream
1 teaspoon salt
½ teaspoon dry mustard

½ teaspoon paprika
¼ teaspoon dried marjoram
⅛ teaspoon freshly ground pepper

Sauté the chicken livers in the butter just until they lose color, then combine with the onion, eggs, and parsley and either chop fine by hand or whir in a blender. Blend with the remaining ingredients, turn into a buttered mold, and chill.

Unmold on a serving plate and garnish as desired.

FAR EAST CHICKEN WINGLETS

⅔ cup cornstarch
½ teaspoon Spice Islands Mei Yen seasoning
Salt and freshly ground pepper to taste
1 egg, lightly beaten
18 chicken wings, cut in two at the second joint and tips discarded
½ cup granulated sugar
2 tablespoons chicken broth or stock
1 clove garlic, put through a press
1 teaspoon soy sauce
2 to 3 teaspoons catsup
⅓ cup vinegar
Butter

Make a batter of the cornstarch, Mei Yen, salt, pepper, and egg. Set it aside. With a small knife, push the chicken meat from the small end to the meaty end of the wing (leaving a kind of "handle"), being careful not to cut through the flesh. In a small saucepan, over low heat, cook the sugar, broth, garlic, soy sauce, catsup, and vinegar, stirring, until the sugar is dissolved and the sauce well blended.

Melt a little butter in a skillet. Dip the wing parts into batter, and when butter is good and hot, brown the wings very lightly. Drain well on paper toweling, then place in a shallow baking pan and pour the sauce over. Bake in a 350° oven, basting frequently, for about 35 minutes, or until all the liquid is absorbed. Serve immediately, allowing generous amounts of cocktail napkins. (It has been my experience that neither a hot tray nor a chafing dish is necessary, as guests seldom allow the winglets to stay around long enough to cool off!)

DILLED CHICKEN DIP

¾ cup ground or finely minced, cooked chicken
¾ cup sour cream
¼ teaspoon salt
Dash of white pepper
1 tablespoon minced onion
½ teaspoon dried dillweed

Whir all the ingredients in a blender until smooth and creamy. Transfer to a serving bowl and surround with Melba toast, shredded wheat biscuits, and carrot or celery sticks.

CHICKEN-ENDIVE PICK-UPS

This appetizer will "wait" for your guests, as endive does not wilt quickly.

2 small heads Belgian endive
1½ cups chicken salad of your choice (see pages 27–32)
Sweet gherkins or sliced, stuffed olives for garnish

Separate and wash the endive leaves, and then pat dry. Fill each leaf generously (but not to the heaping point) with chicken salad. Garnish each with a fan-cut sweet gherkin or overlapping slices of stuffed green olives.

STUFFED EGGS I

1 pound chicken livers
1/3 cup softened butter
6 hard-cooked eggs
Salt and freshly ground pepper to taste
1 1/2 tablespoons sherry

Sauté the chicken livers in a little of the butter until they lose color. Meanwhile, halve the eggs lengthwise. Remove the yolks, reserving 3 for later use in a salad or as a garnish. Setting all the whites aside, put the remaining yolks and the rest of the ingredients into a blender container and whir until smooth. Fill the reserved egg whites with the mixture, using a fancy tip on a pastry bag to flute or simply running the tines of a fork across the filling. Garnish as desired.

STUFFED EGGS II

8 hard-cooked eggs
1 1/4 cups ground or finely minced, cooked chicken
Salt and freshly ground pepper to taste
1/3 cup mayonnaise
1 teaspoon prepared horseradish
1/2 cup finely chopped celery hearts
Watercress or parsley and paprika for garnish

Halve the eggs lengthwise. Remove the yolks and mash with a fork. Setting the whites aside, mix the mashed yolks with the chicken and all the other ingredients except the garnish. Taste for seasoning, and adjust if necessary. Fill the reserved whites with the chicken mixture and top each with a sprig of watercress or parsley and a light dusting of paprika.

PÂTÉ EN GELÉE

2 ten-and-one-half-ounce cans beef bouillon, undiluted
2 envelopes unflavored gelatin
3 teaspoons minced chives
3 teaspoons minced fresh parsley
¼ cup sherry or brandy
1½ cups ground, cooked chicken livers seasoned to taste
Bouquet of watercress or parsley for garnish

Combine the bouillon and gelatin in a saucepan and stir over medium heat until the gelatin dissolves completely. Remove from the heat. Mix together half each of the chives, parsley, and sherry or brandy and blend into the gelatin mixture. Pour into an oiled 3-cup ring mold and refrigerate until firm.

Meanwhile, mix all the other ingredients, except the garnish, thoroughly with the chicken livers. When the gelatin is firm, scoop half of it from the mold, leaving a "shell" on the sides and bottom. Fill the hollowed-out section with the chicken mixture, pressing down lightly. Melt the leftover bouillon-gelatin mixture in a small saucepan and pour it over the chicken in the mold; it will fill in all the empty spots. Chill again until firm.

Unmold on a serving plate, fill the center of the ring with a bouquet of watercress or parsley, and surround with crackers or bread rounds on which to serve the molded pâté slices.

RUMAKI

6 chicken livers
1½ dozen canned water chestnuts
9 slices bacon, halved crosswise
½ cup soy sauce

¾ teaspoon ground ginger
1 clove garlic, put through a press

Cut each liver into thirds and fold each piece around a small water chestnut. (If the chestnuts are too large, simply trim to fit.) Wrap a piece of bacon around the liver-chestnut and secure with a toothpick. Marinate for at least 2 hours in the soy sauce spiced with the ginger and garlic, then place on a rack in a shallow pan and bake in a 425° oven for 10 minutes, or until the bacon is crisp. Remove the toothpicks (which will be charred) and replace with decorative cocktail picks. Serve hot. (*Makes 18 rumaki*)

STONED CHICKEN

1 whole chicken breast
1 small sliced onion
2 tablespoons chopped candied ginger
1½ teaspoons salt
1 cup dry white wine

Combine the chicken, onion, and ginger in a saucepan. Add water to cover and the salt. Bring to a boil, then lower the heat and simmer for about 15 minutes, or until the chicken is tender but firm. Remove the chicken meat from the bone and cut in large cubes (about 1 inch). Place the meat in a small bowl, along with the wine. Cover and refrigerate for several hours—the longer the better. Drain and serve the chicken on decorative picks.

CHICKEN SPREADS AND/OR DIPS

Each of the following should be blended carefully with a fork and spread on cocktail rye bread, thin-sliced white or pumpernickel. Don't use crackers for these, as the spreads have interesting and unusual textures in themselves. Garnish each canapé with sprigs of watercress, parsley, or fancy-cut radish slices. Or, if you prefer to have guests serve themselves, simply spoon the spreads into small, decorative bowls and surround them with various types of bread rounds. Don't forget the spreading knives.

I

¾ cup minced, cooked chicken
⅓ cup crushed pineapple
3 tablespoons mayonnaise

II

½ cup ground, cooked chicken livers
½ cup ground, cooked shrimp
¼ medium onion, minced
Chili sauce to bind

III

1 cup minced, cooked chicken
½ cup chopped, toasted almonds
1 teaspoon grated onion
½ teaspoon curry powder
½ cup mayonnaise

3 Soups

The Life They Save May Be Your Own

Chicken in the whole is *more* than equal to the sum of its parts—not only because the bird is less wearing on the food budget when purchased whole, but because those ignoble parts, the backs, necks and innards, together create the most indispensable item in any home freezer: an ample supply of chicken stock.

Subtly seasoned, gently simmered until it is gloriously golden, chicken stock (or broth or soup) has been known to rescue many a meal from mediocrity. *Always* keep chicken stock in good supply—you'll find it's worth its weight in liquid gold.

Chicken stock freezes well and keeps even better. After simmering it to a rich and heady conclusion, cool it quickly and decant it into as many ice-cube trays as necessary. Pop them into the freezer. When they're frozen solid, flip the cubes out of the trays and slip them into a plastic bag. Squeeze out the air and fasten the neck of the bag tightly with an elastic band or one of those marvelous little paper-wrapped wires. Back into the freezer, and *voilà!* a bagful of instant miracles!

The soups in this chapter are based, for the most part, on the recipe for Starter Chicken Stock (page 16), but you may, of course, use any good chicken stock or broth you wish.

STARTER CHICKEN STOCK

1 four- to five-pound stewing fowl, disjointed
4 to 5 quarts water
5 stalks celery, with leaves, cut up
2 carrots, cut up
1 onion, cut up
1 bay leaf
¼ teaspoon freshly grated nutmeg
Salt and freshly ground pepper to taste

Simmer the chicken in the water, partially covered, for at least 2 hours before adding the vegetables and seasonings. Continue simmering for at least another hour, or until the chicken meat is almost falling off the bones. Taste and adjust the seasoning.

Allow the fowl to cool in its broth, then skin it, bone it, and refrigerate the meat for another dish (salad, dip, croquettes or what you will). Strain the broth and chill it over ice cubes quickly so the fat will coagulate, simplifying its removal, and discard. Pour the broth into ice-cube trays (see page 15) and freeze. (*Makes 4 to 5 quarts*)

VARIATIONS

If serving the broth just as broth, boil a little rice in it. Or add some barley. Or the chopped-up meat of the chicken.

Or be a little different: whip a whole egg in an individual bouillon cup. Continue to beat as you slowly pour over it a cupful of the piping hot broth. Top with a dusting of chopped parsley.

CHICKEN SOUP WITH GUSTO

1 five- to six-pound hen
2 veal knuckles
6 quarts cold water

Salt and freshly ground pepper to taste
2 celery hearts, leaves and all, chopped
6 carrots, peeled and sliced thin
1 large onion, quartered
3 parsnips, peeled and sliced thin
6 to 8 leeks, cleaned and cut into ½-inch pieces
⅛ teaspoon poultry seasoning

Place all the ingredients except the leeks and poultry seasoning in a large soup kettle and bring to a boil. Turn the flame down, cover and simmer for about 2 hours, skimming off the foam from time to time. Add the leeks and poultry seasoning and simmer for another hour, or until the chicken is fork tender.

Let the bird cool in the soup, then skin it, bone it and refrigerate the meat for another dish—there should be enough for a nice-sized casserole (pages 120–134). Strain the soup and chill it so the fat may be removed easily. Serve very hot, with a sprinkling of crumbled French-fried onions on top. Or freeze it all (or part of it) and use as basic stock. (*Serves 10 to 12*)

LUANA'S HONOLULU BISQUE

This is unusual, delicious, and *highly* caloric.

1 quart Starter Chicken Stock (page 16)
1 cup creamy peanut butter
1 cup rich milk or half-and-half
3 tablespoons light rum
½ cup shredded coconut or flaked crabmeat

Heat the chicken stock in a large saucepan. Blend the peanut butter into 1 cup of the hot stock, then stir it into the remainder of the stock in the saucepan, stirring constantly until smooth and creamy. Add the milk and simmer gently for 10 minutes. Taste for seasoning and add the rum.

Serve very hot, with a topping of shredded coconut or flaked crabmeat. (*Serves 4 to 6*)

HEARTY BALKAN-STYLE CHICKEN SOUP

1 five-pound hen, disjointed
4 quarts cold water
Salt and freshly ground pepper to taste
2 carrots, peeled and chopped
2 parsnips, peeled and sliced
2 stalks young celery, sliced
1 medium onion, whole
1 tablespoon butter
½ tablespoon all-purpose flour
Paprika to taste
1 egg yolk beaten with ¼ cup heavy cream

Simmer the chicken in the water, partially covered, for about 1½ hours. Add the salt, pepper, and vegetables and continue simmering until the meat almost falls off the bones. Remove the fowl, then bone and cut the meat into bite-sized pieces. Return the meat to the broth.

In a small saucepan, melt the butter and stir in the flour until it is thoroughly blended and turns a light brown. Add this roux to the soup, stirring well. Allow to simmer for about 5 minutes. Season with paprika, taste, then adjust the seasoning. Just before serving, add the egg yolk–cream mixture, stirring until velvety smooth. Include enough chicken meat in each soup bowl to "go around." (*Serves 8 to 10*)

HUNGARIAN-STYLE CHICKEN SOUP

- 1 five-pound chicken, disjointed
- 4 quarts cold water
- 2 green peppers, seeded and cut into strips
- 10 fresh mushrooms, stems and all, sliced lengthwise
- 1 ten-ounce package frozen peas
- ¼ head green cabbage, shredded
- Salt and freshly ground pepper to taste
- ½ pound thin noodles
- Chopped chives and sour cream for garnish

Put the chicken parts in a soup kettle with the water and bring to a boil; reduce heat and simmer, covered, for 1 hour. Add the vegetables, salt, and pepper and continue simmering until the chicken is tender enough to remove from the bones. Bone it, cut it into bite-sized pieces, and return the meat to soup pot. Meanwhile, in another saucepan, cook the noodles according to package directions. Drain thoroughly and stir into the soup.

Serve the soup in deep bowls, with chopped chives and a dollop of sour cream on top. (*Serves 8 to 10*)

SCOTTISH COCK-A-LEEKIE

- 4 pounds chicken thighs and breasts
- 3 quarts cold water
- 1 celery heart, cut into ½-inch pieces
- 2 white turnips, peeled and diced
- 6 small carrots, peeled and cut up
- 1 onion, stuck with 3 cloves
- 1 small bunch fresh parsley
- 6 medium-sized leeks
- ⅓ cup barley

Cut the chicken breasts into quarters, then put all the ingredients except the leeks and barley into a soup kettle. Bring to boil, then reduce the heat and simmer for about 1½ hours, covered, until the chicken is very tender.

Meanwhile, wash the leeks thoroughly. Discard outer leaves and cut into pieces, including about 1½ inches of the green tops.

When the chicken is tender, remove it from the kettle, bone it, and cut the meat into bite-sized pieces. Strain the soup, reserving the carrots. Put the strained soup back into the kettle over a low flame, add the barley and leeks, and simmer gently for about 30 minutes. Return the carrots and chicken meat to soup and heat thoroughly. (*Serves 8 to 10*)

CHICKEN BISQUE À L'INDIENNE

3 cups Starter Chicken Stock (page 16)
1½ cups peeled, cored, and chopped green pippin apples
1½ cups finely minced onion
⅔ cup heavy cream
¼ teaspoon salt
½ teaspoon curry powder, or to taste

In a saucepan, heat 1½ cups of the stock. Add the apple and onion and simmer until tender, then add the remaining stock and bring to a gentle boil. Lower the heat and cook for 15 minutes, then slowly add the cream and cook gently for 2 minutes. Season with the salt and curry powder, allow to blend over medium heat for another 2 minutes, and serve at once. (*Serves 4*)

COLD AVOCADO-CHICKEN SOUP

1 quart Starter Chicken Stock (page 16)
2 medium-sized avocados, peeled, seeded, and cut up
¼ cup dry sherry
1 cup sour cream
⅓ cup coarsely snipped chives

Put the stock, avocados, and sherry in a blender container and whir until smooth. Chill thoroughly before serving, and top individual bowls or cups of this delectable summer first course with mounds of sour cream and a sprinkling of chives. (*Serves 4 to 6*)

DEEP SOUTH CHICKEN SOUP

2 pounds chicken legs
1 pound chicken wings
½ cup chopped celery
4 green onions, chopped
Salt and freshly ground pepper to taste
1 quart Starter Chicken Stock (page 16)
2 ten-and-one-half-ounce cans cream of asparagus soup
2 soup cans whole milk
1 seventeen-ounce can yams, mashed with a fork

Put the chicken parts, celery, onions, salt, pepper, and stock into a soup kettle. Cover and simmer until the chicken is fork tender (about 1½ hours), then remove the fowl and set aside. Blend the asparagus soup and milk together, then add to the soup kettle. Heat the soup, stirring until smooth, then add the chicken parts and mashed yams and stir to blend. When the soup is very hot, serve with a chicken leg or wing in each deep soup bowl. (*Serves 6 to 8*)

CREAM OF CHICKEN AND SHRIMP SOUP

1 can frozen cream of shrimp soup
1 ten-and-one-half-ounce can cream of chicken soup
2 soup cans half-and-half
1 clove garlic, mashed
½ cup almonds, toasted and chopped

Put both soups into a saucepan and stir to blend. Gradually add the milk, beating with a whisk until velvety smooth, then stir in the garlic. Place over very low heat and simmer for a few minutes so the flavors blend; do *not* allow to come to a boil. Serve garnished with the chopped almonds. *(Serves 4 to 6)*

CHICKEN-CLAM BROTH

2½ cups Starter Chicken Stock (page 16)
2½ cups bottled clam juice
¼ cup whipping cream (optional)
Freshly grated Parmesan cheese
Minced fresh parsley

Heat the stock and clam juice over low heat. If you are not calorie-conscious, whip the cream until it peaks. Serve the broth hot, in cups, adding a peak of whipped cream and dusting with cheese and/or parsley. (*Serves 4 to 6*)

CHICKEN-CLAM SOUP

3 tablespoons butter
6 green onions, sliced thin
1 ten-and-one-half-ounce can cream of chicken soup
1 soup can half-and-half
1 seven-ounce can minced clams, undrained
3 tablespoons dry sherry

Melt the butter in a saucepan and sauté the onions until tender. Add soup, milk, and clams with their juice. Blend, then stir in the sherry and heat until piping. Serve with plain, crisp crackers. (*Serves 4*)

CREAMED CHICKEN AND MUSHROOM SOUP

1 ten-and-one-half-ounce can cream of chicken soup
1 ten-and-one-half-ounce can cream of mushroom soup
2 soup cans half-and-half
½ cup vermicelli, broken into bits
2 hard-cooked eggs, chopped

In a soup pot, blend the chicken and mushroom soups until smooth. Slowly stir in the milk, then place over low heat and simmer gently. Add the vermicelli and continue to cook until the pasta is *just* done (*al dente*). Serve very hot, with a sprinkling of chopped eggs. (*Serves 4*)

CHICKEN-CORN CHOWDER

If you'd like to serve something quite unusual in the soup line, add saffron to the pot while the chicken is cooking. Even without the added virtue of the saffron, however, this soup is excellent and very filling.

4 pounds chicken, whole or parts
1 medium onion, chopped
1 celery heart, chopped
4 quarts Starter Chicken Stock (page 16)
2 ten-ounce packages frozen whole-kernel corn
1 four-ounce package Chinese noodles (not fried)
Salt and freshly ground pepper to taste
⅛ teaspoon saffron (optional)

Bring the chicken, onion, celery, and stock to a slow boil in a large soup kettle; cover, reduce the heat and simmer until vegetables and chicken are tender. Remove the chicken (or parts), bone it, and cut the meat into bite-sized pieces. Set aside.

Add the corn, noodles, and seasonings to the broth, bring to a simmer again, and cook, uncovered, for about 10 minutes. Return chicken to pot and continue simmering *only* until the corn and noodles are cooked through. Do not overcook. (*Serves 8 to 12*)

The following recipes are really meals-in-a-dish—*super soup,* if you will. With either recipe serve quantities of fresh, home-made bread, hot sourdough or biscuits for mopping-up purposes. You'll find these not only desirable but *necessary.*

ROSA'S CHICKEN GUMBO

Butter
2 tablespoons all-purpose flour
5 pounds chicken parts
1½ teaspoons salt
2 medium onions, minced
3 quarts water
2 dozen freshly shucked oysters (although canned or bottled oysters will do)
Freshly ground pepper
½ cup minced fresh parsley
1½ teaspoons gumbo filé powder (on most market shelves)
1½ cups cooked rice

Melt 2 tablespoons butter in a heavy saucepan or Dutch oven. Stir in the flour to make a roux, but do not let it brown. Remove from heat. In a separate skillet, sprinkle the chicken with salt and brown in additional butter, then add the onion and sauté until transparent. Add the water to the roux mixture, using a whisk to blend; then add the browned chicken and onion.

Cover the saucepan and cook over low heat until the chicken is tender (about 1½ hours), then add the oysters, pepper, and parsley and cook until the edges of the oysters curl. Remove from the fire and blend in the gumbo filé powder.

Serve in deep bowls over the hot, cooked rice, adding 2 or 3 oysters to each serving plus 1 or 2 pieces of chicken. (*Serves 8 to 12*)

CHICKEN GUMBO CREOLE

1 large onion, chopped
¼ cup (½ stick) butter
3 tablespoons all-purpose flour
4 quarts Starter Chicken Stock (page 16)
1 five-pound chicken, disjointed
1 one-pound can whole tomatoes
Salt and freshly ground pepper to taste
⅛ teaspoon dried thyme
3 bay leaves
½ cup minced fresh parsley
Dash of cayenne
1 dozen large shrimp, peeled and deveined
2 medium crabs, cleaned and hacked into serving pieces, shell and all
1½ pints oysters, fresh or bottled, undrained
1 ten-ounce package frozen okra, defrosted and cut into 1-inch pieces
2 cups cooked rice

Sauté the onion in the butter until lightly browned, then add the flour and blend to make a roux. Put the roux in a heavy soup kettle and gradually add the chicken broth, stirring constantly. Add the chicken parts, tomatoes, salt, pepper, herbs, and cayenne and cook for 30 to 40 minutes, then add the shrimp and crab and simmer another 30 minutes. Add the oysters with their liquid and the okra. Adjust the seasoning, then continue cooking until the edges of the oysters curl.

Serve in deep bowls over the rice, with equal portions of the chicken and shellfish. (*Serves 8 to 12*)

4 Salads

Luncheon and Otherwise

Rich, filling chicken salads are traditionally served at ladies' luncheons. However, it has been my experience that on a really festive buffet table, where a generous selection of both hot and cold foods is served, these chilly chicken offerings generate enthusiasm among the men as well. The first two recipes could also serve as the perfect prelude to a really light summer supper.

CHICKEN SALAD IN AVOCADOS

1½ cups diced, cooked chicken breast
½ cup bottled French dressing
½ cup mayonnaise
½ cup chopped pecans
¼ cup well-drained crushed pineapple
2 green onions, minced
¼ cup chopped celery
3 medium-sized avocados
1 lemon, cut in half, or juice of 1 lemon, approximately
3 lemon slices and paprika for garnish

Marinate the diced chicken in the French dressing for at least 2 hours, then drain the dressing into another bowl, add the mayonnaise, and blend the two together. Mix in the pecans. Fold into this dressing mixture the chicken, pineapple, onions, and celery. Chill.

Meanwhile, pare the avocados, slice lengthwise, and remove the seeds. At once rub the fruit gently with a cut lemon, or spoon lemon juice over them to prevent discoloration. Just before serving, heap the avocado halves with the chicken salad and decorate with half a slice of lemon dusted with paprika. (*Serves 6*)

CHICKEN CUCUMBER SALAD

2 cups diced, cooked chicken breast
1 cup peeled, seeded, and diced cucumber
¾ cup bottled Green Goddess salad dressing
Cherry tomatoes
Crisp lettuce cups

Reserving the tomatoes for garnish and the lettuce, toss all the other ingredients together and serve, chilled, in the crisp lettuce cups. (*Serves 6 to 8*)

CHINESE SESAME CHICKEN SALAD

2 cups slivered, cooked chicken
Peanut oil
½ cup 2-inch pieces cellophane noodles (bean thread)
2 cups shredded lettuce
½ cup diced green onion
Sesame Oil Dressing (see below)
Toasted sesame seeds

Drop the slivered chicken into very hot oil and fry until golden (about 1 or 2 minutes). Remove from the oil and drain on crumpled paper toweling. Drop the cellophane noodles into the hot oil and stir-fry until crisp (about 1½ minutes), being careful not to let the noodles brown. Skim the noodles from the oil with a slotted spoon and toss with the chicken, lettuce, onion, and dressing. Pile the salad onto a platter and sprinkle with toasted sesame seeds. (*Serves 4*)

SESAME OIL DRESSING

½ teaspoon sesame oil
2 tablespoons Chinese plum sauce (in extremis use plum jelly)
1 tablespoon granulated sugar
1 teaspoon white wine vinegar
½ teaspoon dry mustard

Blend all the ingredients thoroughly.

GINGERED PINEAPPLE CHICKEN SALAD

3 tablespoons sherry
1 cup mayonnaise
2½ cups diced, cooked chicken
1 cup thinly sliced celery
1½ cups well-drained pineapple chunks
¾ cup toasted, slivered almonds
½ cup diced candied ginger
Lettuce leaves

Blend the sherry and mayonnaise, then combine the remaining ingredients, except for the lettuce, and fold into the mayonnaise mixture. Chill well and serve on crisp lettuce leaves. (*Serves 4 to 6*)

CHICKEN, BACON, AND EGG SALAD

- 2 cups diced, cooked chicken
- 8 to 10 slices bacon, broiled crisp, drained, and crumbled
- 1 cup coarsely chopped hard-cooked egg
- 1 cup mayonnaise
- 1 cup peeled, seeded, and coarsely chopped tomatoes
- Spice Islands Beau Monde seasoning
- Shredded lettuce

Blend together the chicken, bacon, and egg. Fold the mixture into the mayonnaise, then carefully fold in the chopped tomatoes. Taste for seasoning. Add enough Beau Monde seasoning to give the salad zip—but remember, bacon is salty! Serve on beds of shredded lettuce and garnish as desired. (*Serves 4 to 6*)

FRUITED CHICKEN SALAD I

- 3 cups diced, cooked chicken breasts
- ½ cup seedless grapes (may be canned)
- 1 eight-ounce can mandarin oranges, drained
- 1 tart apple, cored and diced
- ½ cup halved, toasted almonds
- 1 cup mayonnaise
- Lettuce
- Maraschino cherries for garnish

Combine all ingredients except mayonnaise, lettuce, and cherries, then fold the fruit and chicken mixture into the dressing and chill. Serve on any type of lettuce base and garnish with 2 or 3 maraschino cherries. (*Serves 6 to 8*)

FRUITED CHICKEN SALAD II

- 3 cups diced, cooked chicken breasts
- 1 cup diced ham
- 1¼ cups seedless grapes (may be canned)

1¼ cups coarsely chopped macadamia nuts
½ cup chopped celery
Salt and freshly ground pepper to taste
1¼ teaspoons monosodium glutamate
¼ cup finely snipped chives
2 hard-cooked eggs, diced
1 cup mayonnaise
Watercress

Combine all the ingredients except the watercress, blending in the mayonnaise last. Taste for seasoning, then serve on a bed of watercress. (*Serves 6 to 8*)

CHICKEN-APPLE SALAD

3 cups diced, cooked chicken
1 cup thinly sliced celery
1 cup coarsely chopped walnuts
2 cups unpeeled, cored, and diced tart red apples
1½ cups mayonnaise
12 prunes or dates, pitted
Softened cream cheese
Boston or Bibb lettuce

Lightly toss together all the ingredients except the dates, cream cheese, and lettuce. Mound on a bed of the lettuce. Stuff the pitted fruit with the cream cheese and use as a garnish. (*Serves 6 to 8*)

JENNIFER'S PRIDE

- ¾ cup mayonnaise
- ¼ cup sour cream
- 3 cups diced, cooked chicken breast
- 1½ cups thinly sliced celery
- ½ cup sliced ripe olives
- ½ cup toasted, slivered almonds
- ¼ cup finely snipped chives
- Salt and freshly ground pepper to taste
- Crisp lettuce

Blend the mayonnaise and sour cream and set aside to allow the flavors to meld. Combine the remaining ingredients, except for the lettuce, and taste for seasoning. Add the mayonnaise–sour cream, blend lightly, and chill before serving on crisp lettuce. (*Serves 6 to 8*)

CHICKEN CHUTNEY SALAD

- ⅔ cup mayonnaise
- 2 teaspoons Dijon mustard
- Salt and freshly ground pepper to taste
- ¾ cup good-quality chutney (I prefer Major Grey's)
- 2½ cups cubed, cooked chicken
- 8 sweet gherkins
- 12 thin slices cucumber, halved
- ⅔ cup chopped salted, roasted peanuts

Mix together the mayonnaise, mustard, salt, and pepper. Drain the syrup from the chutney and set aside. Cut the chutney fruit into very tiny pieces, then pour the reserved syrup over. Combine the chutney with the mayonnaise mixture, and when thoroughly blended, fold in the cubed chicken. Serve well chilled, garnished with the gherkins, a few cucumber slices, and an overall sprinkling of chopped peanuts. (*Serves 6*)

MACARONI-CHICKEN SALAD

- **2/3 cup mayonnaise**
- **1/3 cup sour cream**
- **Salt and freshly ground pepper to taste**
- **2 cups cooked, drained elbow macaroni, well-rinsed**
- **1 cup diced, cooked chicken meat**
- **1/2 cup diced, cooked ham**
- **1/3 cup slivered green pepper**
- **1/3 cup thinly sliced celery**
- **4 green onions, green part and all, minced**
- **2/3 cup diced sharp Tillamook cheese**
- **Small lettuce leaves for garnish**

Combine the mayonnaise, sour cream, salt and pepper. In a separate bowl, combine all the other ingredients except the cheese and lettuce. Fold the mayonnaise mixture into the chicken mixture, and when thoroughly combined, turn into a chilled bowl. Sprinkle the top with the cheese and edge the bowl with the small lettuce leaves. (*Serves 6 to 8*)

MEDALLION OF CHICKEN ASPIC

- **2 tablespoons butter**
- **2 tablespoons all-purpose flour**
- **1 cup light cream**
- **1 1/2 envelopes unflavored gelatin**
- **1/2 cup cold water**
- **8 slices cooked chicken breast**
- **8 slices boiled ham**
- **2 hard-cooked egg yolks**
- **1/4 cup sour cream**
- **Salt and freshly ground pepper to taste**
- **Watercress and sliced, stuffed green olives for garnish**

Heat the butter in a small saucepan and blend in the flour.

Add the cream and cook, stirring, until thickened and smooth. Soften the gelatin in the cold water, then dissolve it in the hot white sauce, stirring constantly. Allow to cool, then chill until thickened. Meanwhile, using a biscuit cutter, cut rounds from the chicken and ham slices. Cover the chicken rounds with a little of the aspic, and top with the ham rounds. Set aside.

Into a blender container, put the scraps of chicken and ham (left from the cutting out of the rounds), egg yolks, and sour cream. Whir until the mixture is very smooth, then add salt and pepper. Taste for seasoning and adjust, if necessary. Using a steel-bladed spatula, mound the sour cream mixture carefully over the chicken-ham-aspic mounds and refrigerate until set.

If the remaining gelatin mixture is too thick to work with, heat very slowly until it reaches a good, spreadable consistency. "Ice" the mounds with the aspic and chill again. Garnish each chicken/ham mound with watercress and a ring of sliced, stuffed olives. (*Serves 6 to 8*)

PEACHY CHICKEN MOLDS

1½ envelopes unflavored gelatin
1¾ cups cranberry juice
3 tablespoons granulated sugar
½ teaspoon grated orange rind
½ teaspoon grated lemon rind
¼ cup orange juice
1 tablespoon lemon juice
¾ cup diced celery
2½ cups diced, cooked chicken breast
Chopped lettuce or watercress
6 large spiced peaches, stoned and halved
Mayonnaise

Soften the gelatin in 1 cup of the cranberry juice. Add the sugar and heat slowly over a low flame until the gelatin is dissolved, stirring constantly. Add the orange and lemon rind, the orange and lemon juices, and the remaining ¾ cup of cranberry juice. Blend well and chill until the mixture is not *quite* firm, then fold in the celery and chicken. Pour into individual, oiled molds and chill until very firm.

When ready to serve, unmold on chopped lettuce or a bed of watercress. Place a spiced peach half on either side of each mold. Mayonnaise is sufficient dressing for this salad. (*Serves 6*)

CHICKEN SOUP-IN-A-SALAD

- **1 cup cold water**
- **2 envelopes unflavored gelatin**
- **1 ten-and-one-half-ounce can cream of asparagus soup, undiluted**
- **¾ cup mayonnaise**
- **¼ cup bottled Italian dressing**
- **2 tablespoons lemon juice**
- **2 teaspoons minced green onion**
- **2½ cups diced, cooked chicken**
- **1 cup chopped celery**
- **1 four-ounce jar pimiento, cut in strips**
- **Watercress for garnish**

Put the cold water in a saucepan and sprinkle the gelatin over it. When softened, heat over a low flame, stirring constantly, until the gelatin is completely dissolved. Remove the pan from the fire and blend in the soup, mayonnaise, Italian dressing, lemon juice, and onion. Beat with a rotary beater until the mixture is very smooth, then place the saucepan in a large bowl of ice and stir the mixture constantly until it drops in mounds from the spoon. Fold in the chicken and celery and spoon into an oiled loaf pan. Chill until firm.

When ready to serve, unmold on a decorative serving platter and garnish with the pimiento strips and watercress. (*Serves 6 to 8*)

MISH-MASH CHICKEN MOLD

3 envelopes unflavored gelatin
1½ cups cold rich chicken broth
2 cups mayonnaise
2 tablespoons Worcestershire sauce
2 cups diced celery
1 cup chopped pecans
1 twelve-ounce can tiny French peas
3 tablespoons India relish or sweet pickle relish
4 cups diced, cooked chicken breast

In a saucepan, soften the gelatin in the cold chicken broth, then heat over a low flame, stirring constantly, until the gelatin dissolves. Remove from the fire and stir in the mayonnaise and Worcestershire sauce. Allow to cool until it begins to thicken, then add the remaining ingredients, the chicken last of all. Chill thoroughly in an oiled loaf pan or a mold, then unmold and garnish with whatever appeals to your artistic nature—radish roses, pimiento strips, or sliced, stuffed olives. (*Serves 6 to 8*)

MOLDED CHICKEN CURRY SALAD

2 envelopes unflavored gelatin
1 cup cold rich chicken broth
2 eggs, separated
3 teaspoons Indian curry powder

¼ teaspoon salt
1½ cups cottage cheese, whipped in a blender
2 tablespoons lemon juice
⅓ cup chopped chutney
2 teaspoons minced green onion
2½ cups diced, cooked chicken
½ cup heavy cream
Shredded coconut, pecan halves, finely minced chives, and kumquats or curly endive for garnish

In a saucepan, soften the gelatin in the cold chicken broth. Add the egg yolks and mix thoroughly, then heat over a low flame, stirring constantly, until the mixture begins to thicken. Remove from the heat and stir in the curry powder and salt. Blend in the cottage cheese, then add the lemon juice, chutney, onion, and chicken, mixing lightly but well. Chill.

Meanwhile whip the egg whites until they peak and whip the cream until it peaks. Gently fold both into chicken mixture, then transfer carefully to a large, oiled ring mold and chill until very firm.

When ready to serve, unmold onto a platter and sprinkle the salad with coconut. Wreath the top with pecan halves and and color with a dusting of finely minced chives. Surround with kumquats or curly endive. (*Serves 6*)

5 Breasts

Just the White Meat, Please!

Please don't take this chapter heading as a personal comment. When it comes to chicken, I am totally color-blind. For me there is no "best" piece. Yet one cannot ignore those epicurean bigots who stubbornly deny their palates the succulent pleasures of thigh or drumstick, and it is to them that I dedicate the following.

Although one good-sized chicken breast traditionally serves two, I have found that most young supermarket birds, not being as well developed as their elders, yield only enough for a single serving. It may be that my friends boast exaggerated appetites; nevertheless, I suggest you buy chicken breasts as "parts" and allow two halves per serving.

CHICKEN BREASTS IN CHAMPAGNE

6 chicken breasts, halved, skinned, and boned
1/3 cup all-purpose flour, mixed with salt and freshly ground pepper to taste
1/4 cup (1/2 stick) butter
4 shallots, minced

¾ cup champagne (a split should do nicely)
¾ cup rich chicken broth
12 mushrooms, sliced thin
⅓ cup sour cream

Dust the chicken breasts lightly with the seasoned flour. Melt the butter in a heavy skillet and brown the chicken on both sides. Remove the chicken from the skillet and set aside, then lightly brown the shallots in the same pan. Add the champagne, the browned chicken, cover, and simmer for 15 minutes. Add the broth and simmer until chicken is tender—perhaps another 10 to 15 minutes. Add the mushrooms and cook for 5 minutes longer.

Remove the chicken to a hot platter, and over *very* low heat, add the sour cream to the sauce. Stir until well blended, then spoon over the chicken breasts and serve. (*Serves 6*)

KATINKA'S CHICKEN APRICOT

6 chicken breasts, halved
1½ cups water, well seasoned with salt and freshly ground pepper
1 twenty-nine-ounce can apricot halves
1 cup apricot nectar
5 tablespoons brandy

For this type of recipe, I generally cook the chicken breasts in a pressure cooker with 1½ cups water, timing 8 minutes after the pressure has been reached. This facilitates skinning and boning the breasts, and also yields a fair amount of excellent stock, which I season well.

After the breasts are cooked, skinned, and boned, place them in a single layer in a suitable casserole, then lay the apricot halves on top. Combine the apricot nectar and the broth (from the pressure cooker) and pour over the chicken.

Cover and bake in a 350° oven for about 15 to 20 minutes, or long enough to heat the dish through. Just before serving, stir in the brandy. (*Serves 6*)

CHICKEN BREASTS CALORIC

2 cups sour cream
1 package onion soup mix
1 cup whipping cream
2 bunches broccoli, divided into spears and cooked
8 chicken breasts, halved, skinned, and boned
⅓ cup freshly grated, mixed Parmesan and Romano cheese

Combine the sour cream, soup mix, and unwhipped whipping cream in a saucepan and heat slowly, stirring with care, until hot but not bubbling. Place the cooked broccoli spears, heads to stalks to make an even layer, in a shallow casserole or baking dish. Pour half the sauce over the broccoli, then lay the chicken breasts on top and pour the remainder of the sauce over them. Bake in a 350° oven for 15 minutes, then sprinkle cheese generously over all and bake another 15 to 20 minutes, or until the sauce is bubbly and the cheese is golden brown. (*Serves 8*)

STUFFED CHICKEN BREASTS

⅓ to ½ cup melted butter
¾ cup canned pie apples, drained and chopped
½ cup chopped pecans
⅓ cup crushed, drained pineapple
½ cup raisins
¾ teaspoon ground cinnamon
¼ teaspoon ground ginger

¾ cup crushed herbed croutons
4 whole chicken breasts, halved and boned
¾ teaspoon salt

Combine ¼ cup of the melted butter with all the other ingredients except the chicken and salt and stir until well blended. Sprinkle the undersides of the breasts with the salt, then divide the crumb mixture into 8 equal parts and place each on the underside of a breast. Fold each breast crosswise, gently, and secure with toothpicks or small skewers.

Use remaining butter to grease a fairly shallow baking dish. Put the chicken breasts in the dish, then place in a 350° oven and bake for approximately 25 minutes. Turn the breasts over and continue baking for another 20 minutes, or until pieces are tender and golden. If they appear to be drying out, drizzle a little more melted butter over them from time to time.

Note: This recipe proves the exception to our rule of breasts: prepared this way, 4 whole breasts should serve 8.

CHICKEN BREASTS KAMEHAMEHA

½ cup all-purpose flour
Salt, freshly ground pepper, and monosodium glutamate to taste
8 chicken breasts, halved and boned
16 pineapple fingers or 8 pineapple spears, halved
½ cup pine nuts
1 cup evaporated milk
2 tablespoons peanut oil
¼ cup (½ stick) butter
¾ cup grated coconut

Mix together flour and seasonings. Wrap each halved chicken breast around a pineapple finger sprinkled with pine nuts.

Secure with toothpicks or small skewers, then dip each roll in evaporated milk, then in the flour mixture. Chill for 2 hours.

When ready to cook, heat the oil and butter together in a large frying pan and brown the chicken rolls lightly. Have ready a buttered, shallow baking pan or dish. Arrange the rolls in it, sprinkle them with the grated coconut, and bake in a 350° oven for about 30 minutes, or until the chicken is tender when pierced with a fork. Arrange the chicken rolls on a platter and spoon the pan juices over. (*Serves 8*)

CHICKEN BREASTS BISTRO

½ cup all-purpose flour
Salt, freshly ground pepper, and monosodium glutamate to taste
8 chicken breasts, halved, boned, and skinned
2 to 3 tablespoons butter
1 eight-ounce can water chestnuts, drained and sliced
1 ten-and-one-half-ounce can cream of chicken soup
¾ cup white port wine
¼ cup minced watercress
Watercress clusters for garnish

Combine the flour and seasonings, then dredge the chicken in the mixture. Lightly brown chicken in the butter, then transfer to a greased, shallow baking dish and top with the water chestnuts. Blend the soup and wine and pour over the chicken. Bake, uncovered, in a 325° oven for 50 to 60 minutes, or until the chicken breasts are fork tender. To serve, sprinkle with minced watercress and garnish with a few whole clusters of the cress. (*Serves 8*)

CHICKEN BREASTS JAPANESE

1 one-and-one-half-ounce package dried Japanese or Chinese mushrooms
1 cup cold water
½ cup all-purpose flour
Salt and freshly ground pepper to taste
1½ teaspoons monosodium glutamate
6 chicken breasts, halved, boned, and skinned
⅓ cup butter
⅓ cup minced onion
⅔ cup dry white wine

Soak the mushrooms in the water according to package directions. Meanwhile, combine the flour with the salt, pepper, and monosodium glutamate and dredge the chicken in the mixture. Melt the butter in a large frying pan and brown the chicken lightly in butter, then push the chicken to one side while you cook the onion until it is transparent.

Squeeze all the water from the soaked mushrooms and cut into pieces with kitchen shears. Spread the mushrooms over the chicken and add the wine, then cover and simmer gently over a low flame for about 35 minutes, or until the fowl is fork tender. (*Serves 6*)

CHINA CITY CHICKEN BREASTS

- 6 chicken breasts, halved, boned, and skinned
- ½ teaspoon salt
- 2 tablespoons cornstarch
- 3 cloves garlic, halved
- ¼ cup peanut oil
- 1 eight-ounce can pineapple chunks, drained but liquid reserved
- 1 four-ounce jar mixed sweet pickles, chopped and drained but liquid reserved
- 1 tablespoon soy sauce
- ½ green pepper, cut into strips
- 1 twelve-ounce can preserved kumquats, drained

Cut the chicken breasts into narrow strips. Combine the salt and half the cornstarch and roll the chicken strips in the mixture. Spear the garlic pieces with toothpicks (for easy removal from the fat) and sauté in the oil in a large frying pan or wok for 1 minute, then remove the garlic and discard. Add the chicken to the pan and stir-fry for 2 minutes over high heat. Add the reserved pineapple juice, liquid from the pickles, and soy sauce and blend quickly but thoroughly. Bring just to a boil, then add the pineapple chunks, chopped pickles, and pepper strips. Dissolve the remaining cornstarch in an equal amount of water, then stir into the juices in pan until they are thickened. (Do this quickly so that the pepper strips are still slightly crunchy.) Garnish with the preserved kumquats and serve with plain boiled or steamed rice. (*Serves 8; 10 with a stretch*)

CHICKEN BREASTS POMPADOUR

- ¼ cup (½ stick) butter
- 4 chicken breasts, halved, boned, and skinned

1/3 cup good Burgundy
1/3 cup red currant jelly
Salt and freshly ground pepper to taste

Melt the butter in a large skillet and lightly brown the chicken on both sides, then lower the heat and cook for 6 minutes. Add the wine and jelly, stirring well until the jelly melts. Season to taste.

To serve, spoon the sauce over chicken. (*Serves 4*)

BREAST OF CHICKEN SAUVAGE

2 cups raw wild rice
1 quart strong chicken broth
3 chicken breasts, halved, boned, and skinned
1/2 cup (1 stick) butter
1/2 cup seedless raisins
1/2 cup orange juice
3 tablespoons all-purpose flour
1/2 teaspoon paprika
Salt and freshly ground pepper to taste
1 1/2 cups light cream or half-and-half

Measure the rice into a large strainer and wash thoroughly under cold water. Add to chicken broth in a saucepan, cover, and bring to a boil. Uncover, then simmer, stirring from time to time, until the rice is done and the liquid is absorbed—about 45 minutes.

Meanwhile, brown the chicken on both sides in the butter, then cover and cook over low heat for about 30 or 35 minutes, or until the chicken yields easily to a fork. While the chicken is cooking, combine the raisins with the orange juice in a small saucepan and bring to a boil. Simmer for 5 minutes, then set the raisins aside.

Remove the chicken from pan and pour off all but 3 tablespoons fat. Stir in the flour, paprika, salt and pepper, then add the cream and cook over low heat, stirring constantly, until smooth and thickened. Taste for seasoning and adjust, if necessary. Stir in the reserved raisin mixture.

Arrange 6 mounds of rice in a shallow, buttered baking dish. Place a chicken breast on each and top with sauce. Bake in a 350° oven for 10 minutes. (*Serves 6*)

WINE-BAKED CHICKEN BREASTS

3 large chicken breasts, halved and boned but skin left intact
Salt and freshly ground pepper to taste
3 tablespoons all-purpose flour
3 tablespoons light cream or half-and-half
1 cup sour cream
1 ten-and-one-half-ounce can cream of chicken soup, undiluted
½ cup dry sherry, more if necessary
8 fresh mushrooms, sliced and sautéed in butter
¾ cup toasted, slivered almonds

Place the chicken breasts in a single layer, skin side up, in a shallow, buttered baking dish, then sprinkle with the salt and pepper. Combine the flour and cream and blend until smooth, then stir in the sour cream. Add the soup and sherry and stir until the mixture is creamy-smooth.

Scatter the mushrooms over the chicken and pour the sauce over all. Add the nuts, sprinkling evenly over the top of the dish, and bake in a 325° oven for about 35 to 40 minutes, or until the chicken is tender. (If the liquid cooks away, add a little more sherry.) (*Serves 6*)

CHEESE- AND HAM-STUFFED BREASTS

4 chicken breasts, halved, boned, and skinned
8 thin slices Swiss or Gruyère cheese
8 thin slices boiled ham
1 cup commercially prepared seasoned bread crumbs

Lay the chicken breasts between two sheets of waxed paper and pound with a wooden mallet or the side of a cleaver. Be careful not to break the meat, but pound until the breasts are thin and pliable. Top each piece with one slice of cheese and one of ham, then roll and secure with toothpicks or small skewers. Dredge each breast in the seasoned crumbs and place in an ungreased shallow pan. Bake in a 400° oven for about 30 minutes, keeping a watchful eye on the breasts so they don't become too brown. (They should emerge from the oven crusty outside and moistly delicious within.) (*Serves 4*)

CHEESY CHICKEN WITH ASPARAGUS

1 ten-and-one-half-ounce can Cheddar cheese soup, undiluted
1 cup light cream or half-and-half
½ cup sour cream
2 tablespoons sherry
6 slices white bread, toasted and cut in half diagonally
2 to 2½ pounds fresh asparagus, cooked
6 generous slices cooked chicken breast
¾ cup freshly grated Parmesan cheese

In the top of a double boiler, blend together the soup, half-and-half, sour cream, and sherry; place over boiling water to keep hot. Place the toast triangles in a large, shallow baking pan and cover with the cooked asparagus. Lay the chicken slices over the asparagus, then pour the hot cheese sauce over all. Sprinkle with the Parmesan cheese and bake in a 350° oven until the top is bubbly and lightly browned. (*Serves 6*)

CHICKEN-MUSHROOM CASSEROLE

6 tablespoons (¾ stick) butter
4 chicken breasts, halved and boned
1 bunch leeks, cleaned well and cut in ¼-inch slices, including part of the green
½ pound mushrooms, sliced
2 ten-and-one-half-ounce cans cream of chicken soup, undiluted
¾ cup light cream or half-and-half
Salt and freshly ground pepper to taste
¼ teaspoon dried rosemary

Melt the butter in a large frying pan and lightly brown the chicken, then remove it to a shallow, buttered casserole. Cook the leeks for 5 minutes in the remaining butter in the pan, then add the mushrooms and cook an additional 5 minutes, stirring occasionally. Place the vegetables around chicken.

Blend together the soup and cream and pour over the contents of the casserole. Add salt and pepper, then crumble the rosemary over the dish and bake in a 350° oven for about 30 to 35 minutes, or until the chicken is tender. (*Serves 6 to 8*)

NOODLES AND CHICKEN BREASTS

6 tablespoons (¾ stick) butter
3 chicken breasts, halved and boned
Salt and freshly ground pepper to taste

½ pound mushrooms, sliced
1 cup light cream or half-and-half
2 tablespoons arrowroot
½ cup sherry
3½ to 4 cups cooked noodles
Paprika

Melt 4 tablespoons of the butter in a deepish flameproof baking pan. Turn the chicken breasts in it until they are well coated, then season to taste with salt and pepper. Cover the pan with foil and bake in a 350° oven for about 10 minutes.

Meanwhile, melt the remaining butter in a frying pan and sauté the mushrooms in it for 3 minutes. In a small bowl, combine 2 tablespoons of the cream with the arrowroot and stir until smooth. Set aside. Pour the remaining cream and the sherry into the pan with the mushrooms and season to taste. Stirring carefully, add the arrowroot mixture and cook until well blended.

Remove the chicken from the baking pan. Spread the cooked noodles over the bottom of the pan, replace the chicken, and pour the mushroom sauce over all. Pop back into the oven just long enough to heat through, then dust with paprika. (*Serves 6*)

Note: The dish may be topped with freshly grated Parmesan cheese for added interest.

NUT-BAKED CHICKEN BREASTS

4 large chicken breasts, halved, boned, and skinned
Salt and freshly ground pepper to taste
All-purpose flour
1 egg, well beaten
1½ cups ground macadamia nuts
Freshly grated nutmeg

1/4 cup minced green onions
1/4 cup minced fresh parsley
8 pats of butter (about 1 tablespoon each)

Place the chicken breasts between two sheets of waxed paper and flatten slightly with a mallet or the side of a cleaver, then season well and dust with flour. Dip each breast in the beaten egg, then roll in the ground nuts. Place each breast half on a square of foil, grate a little fresh nutmeg over each, and sprinkle with 1/2 tablespoon each onion and parsley. Top with a pat of butter. Fold and seal edges of the foil and bake in a 375° oven for about 30 minutes, or until tender. (*Serves 8*)

6 Thighs and Drumsticks

Leg Watching Among Friends

All children love drumsticks—including legions of grown-up kids—but for my money there is nothing more satisfying than a nice plump thigh. So this chapter devotes itself to the leg, the whole leg, and nothing but the leg.

FRUIT-STUFFED THIGHS

- **8 chicken thighs, boned**
- **Salt to taste**
- **1 tablespoon dehydrated minced onion**
- **16 dried apricot halves**
- **½ cup toasted, slivered almonds**
- **Hot, cooked rice**
- **½ cup sour cream**
- **6 tablespoons apricot jam**
- **1 tablespoon dark prepared mustard**

Place the boned thighs skin side down on a cutting board, and sprinkle with salt and the onion. Place 2 apricot halves and about 1 tablespoon slivered almonds in the center of each thigh. Fold the sides over and fasten with small bamboo skewers. Place the rolls, seam side down, in a foil-lined baking pan and bake in a 400° oven for 40 to 45 minutes.

Serve on rice, with a sauce made by combining the sour cream, apricot jam, and mustard and heating *just* to the boil. (*Serves 4*)

CHEESE-MARINATED THIGHS

2 tablespoons water
2 tablespoons blue cheese salad dressing mix
⅔ cup corn, peanut, or safflower oil
Juice and grated rind of 1 lemon
8 chicken thighs

Mix the 2 tablespoons water with the salad dressing mix, oil, and lemon rind and juice and pour over the chicken in a shallow dish. Marinate for at least 2 hours (preferably longer).

When ready to cook, broil about 6 inches from the source of heat for about 10 minutes on each side, or until the thighs are nicely browned. Baste frequently with the marinade. (*Serves 4*)

HAM-STUFFED THIGHS

8 chicken thighs, boned
8 slices cooked ham, each about 2 x 1 x 1 inches
1 egg, lightly beaten
Fine, dry bread crumbs
Melted butter

With the skin side down, pound the thighs to flatten them. Center a slice of ham on each and secure by folding the chicken over, pulling the skin to cover, and securing with short bamboo skewers. Dip in the egg, roll in crumbs, and place in a shallow baking dish. Drizzle with melted butter, cover, and bake in a 325° oven for about 1 hour, adding a little more melted butter if the thighs seem to need additional lubrication. Remove the skewers before serving. (*Serves 4 to 6*)

THIGHS À LA RUSSE

8 chicken thighs
1 teaspoon salt
2 four-and-one-half-ounce cans chopped mushrooms, drained but liquid reserved
1 tablespoon minced green onion
Chopped fresh parsley
¼ teaspoon dried thyme
½ cup chopped onion
1 clove garlic, minced or put through a press
3 tablespoons butter
1 beef bouillon cube
2 tablespoons all-purpose flour
¼ cup water
1 cup sour cream
6 ounces long-grained and wild rice mix (uncooked weight), cooked

Bone the thighs, place skin side down on a board, and sprinkle with salt. Mix 1 can of the mushrooms with the green onion, 1 tablespoon chopped parsley, and the thyme. Place 1 tablespoon of the mixture on each thigh, fold over and secure with short bamboo skewers.

Sauté the onion, garlic, and remaining mushrooms in 1 tablespoon of the butter until the onion is lightly golden. Set the mixture aside while you sauté the thighs in the remaining butter until brown, then add to the thighs, along with the mushroom liquid and the bouillon cube. Cover and simmer for 15 minutes.

Meanwhile, combine the flour with the 1/4 cup water, stir in well, bring to a boil, and simmer for 5 minutes. Gently stir in the sour cream and heat through; do *not* boil, or the sour cream will curdle. Remove the skewers and serve the thighs and sauce on a bed of the rice, garnished with additional chopped parsley. (*Serves 4 to 6*)

CHICKEN MOLÉ IN A HURRY

- **2 tablespoons vegetable oil**
- **8 chicken thighs**
- **1/4 cup slivered almonds**
- **1/3 cup chopped green pepper**
- **1/4 cup chopped onion**
- **1/4 cup water**
- **1 clove garlic, put through a press**
- **1 one-pound can chili con carne with beans**
- **2 teaspoons grated unsweetened chocolate**
- **Good pinch of ground cinnamon**
- **Pinch of ground cloves**

Heat the oil in a large frying pan and brown the chicken and almonds. Pour off the excess fat, then add the green pepper, onion, water, and garlic. Cover and cook over low heat for 30 minutes, turning the chicken occasionally. Add the chili, chocolate, and spices, cover, and cook another 15 minutes. (*Serves 4*)

CHICKEN THIGHS EN CROÛTE

For a party, these thigh packets may be prepared ahead, up to the time of baking.

- **6 commercially prepared, frozen patty shells**
- **6 plump chicken thighs**
- **6 thick slices boiled ham**

6 thick slices Swiss cheese
1 ten-and-one-half-ounce can Cheddar cheese soup, undiluted
1/3 cup whole milk
1 cup grated sharp Cheddar cheese
2 teaspoons Worcestershire sauce

Unwrap the patty shells and allow to defrost completely. Do *not* remove the inner circle scored on each shell. Cook the chicken thighs (a pressure cooker comes in handy here), then skin and bone them. (If the thighs lose their shape during deboning, don't despair; the aesthetic "damage" will ultimately be hidden under puff pastry and sauce.) Stack the ham slices and cut into 6 finger-sized lengths, then repeat the procedure with the Swiss cheese.

Roll out each patty shell on a lightly floured board; it must be large enough to enfold a thigh wrapped around the fingers of ham and cheese. Pinch the pastry seams together and arrange each packet, seam side down, on a cookie sheet. Bake according to the directions on the patty shell package.

While the baking process is underway, heat the undiluted soup with the milk. Add the cheese and Worcestershire sauce and stir until well blended. When the pastry is done, serve at once under a blanket of cheese sauce. (*Serves 6*)

DUTCH-OVEN THIGHS

2/3 cup butter, more if necessary
1/2 pound mushrooms, halved
8 small white onions, peeled
8 small new potatoes, peeled
1/2 cup all-purpose flour
Salt and freshly ground pepper to taste
1 teaspoon paprika
8 chicken thighs
2 tablespoons minced parsley

Heat half the butter in a Dutch oven and sauté the mushrooms until golden, then remove from the pot. In the same fat, sauté the onions until lightly browned; remove from the pot. Heat the remaining butter in a skillet and brown the potatoes.

Combine the flour, salt, pepper, and paprika and dredge the thighs in the mixture. Reheat the butter in the Dutch oven and sauté the thighs until they are golden brown, adding more butter if necessary, and sprinkling with about 1 teaspoon salt. Add the mushrooms, onion, and potatoes to the chicken, cover, and cook over low heat, stirring from time to time, for about 20 minutes, or until both chicken and potatoes are tender. Sprinkle with the parsley before serving. (*Serves 6 to 8*)

ITALIAN THIGHS

8 chicken thighs, boned
1 teaspoon salt
1 teaspoon dehydrated minced onion
1 teaspoon chopped fresh parsley
¼ pound mozzarella cheese
½ pound spaghettini or coiled capellini
2 eight-ounce cans tomato sauce
½ teaspoon dried sweet basil
½ teaspoon dried oregano
Freshly grated Parmesan cheese

Place the boned thighs, skin side down on a board, and sprinkle with the salt, onion, and parsley. Cut the mozzarella into 8 equal pieces and place one in the center of each thigh. Fold the thighs over and secure with short bamboo skewers, then place, seam sides down, in a foil-lined baking dish. Bake in a 400° oven for about 40 minutes.

Meanwhile, cook the spaghettini as directed on the

package. Combine the tomato sauce and herbs in a small saucepan and heat.

To serve, make a bed of hot pasta in a deep, hot platter, top with the chicken, and pour the tomato sauce over all. Serve with freshly grated Parmesan cheese on the side. (*Serves 4 to 6*)

SPANISH THIGHS

8 chicken thighs, boned
1 teaspoon salt
3 tablespoons butter
2 tablespoons orange juice
2 tablespoons chopped fresh parsley
1 tablespoon minced chives
Hot cooked rice
Thin orange slices for garnish

Place the boned thighs between two pieces of foil and pound with a mallet or rolling pin until they are like thin cutlets. Sprinkle with the salt, then cook, skin side down, in bubbling butter for about 10 minutes. Turn, sprinkle with the orange juice, parsley, and chives, and cook another 10 minutes, or until tender. Serve on hot rice and garnish with orange slices. (*Serves 4 to 6*)

DRUMSTICKS OHIO

- ½ cup all-purpose flour
- 2 teaspoons salt
- ½ teaspoon freshly ground pepper
- 2 teaspoons paprika
- 8 chicken drumsticks
- ¼ cup (½ stick) butter
- 2 cups cold water
- 2 onions, sliced
- 4 carrots, peeled and sliced thin
- 1 cup chopped celery
- 1 cup chopped green pepper

Combine the flour, salt, pepper, and paprika in a paper bag, pop the drumsticks in, a couple at a time, and shake well until they are nicely coated. Set any remaining flour mixture aside.

Brown the legs in hot, bubbling butter, then carefully stir in the remaining flour mixture and the water, using a whisk if it tends to lump. Cook, covered, over medium heat for about 30 minutes, then add the vegetables and cook for another 15 minutes, or until the chicken is fork tender. (*Serves 4 to 6*)

DRUMSTICKS AU VIN

- 12 chicken drumsticks
- Salt and freshly ground pepper to taste
- 2 tablespoons vegetable oil
- ¼ cup (½ stick) butter
- 1½ cups dry white wine
- 1 cup water
- ½ cup sliced green onions
- 1 four-and-one-half-ounce can sliced mushrooms
- 1 package precooked chicken-flavored rice

Season the chicken with salt and pepper and brown on all sides in the hot oil and 2 tablespoons of the butter. Add half the wine, then cover and simmer until the chicken is tender (about 30 minutes). In a separate saucepan, bring the remaining wine, the water, the remaining butter, the onions, and mushrooms to a boil. Stir in the seasoned rice, cover tightly, and remove from the heat. Let stand for 7 minutes.

To serve, turn the hot rice onto a serving platter and top with the drumsticks. (*Serves 6 to 8*)

PINEAPPLE DRUMSTICKS

6 chicken drumsticks
1 cup pineapple juice
¼ cup lemon juice
1 cup all-purpose flour
1 teaspoon salt
¼ teaspoon paprika
Dash of freshly ground pepper
1 cup half-and-half
2 eggs, well beaten
1 cup flaked coconut
3 tablespoons vegetable oil

Place the drumsticks in a shallow bowl, add the pineapple and lemon juices, and refrigerate for 2 hours.

When ready to cook, combine the flour, salt, paprika, and pepper. Remove the drumsticks from the marinade and dredge in the seasoned flour. Add the half-and-half to the eggs and blend. Dip the chicken into the mixture, then roll in the coconut.

Heat the oil until almost smoking in a large, heavy skillet. Add the chicken, then lower the heat and cook slowly, uncovered, for about 25 to 30 minutes, turning once. Drain and serve hot or cold. (*Serves 4 to 6*)

PARTY DRUMSTICKS

1 seven-ounce bag corn chips
¼ cup freshly grated Parmesan cheese
1 egg, lightly beaten
¾ cup evaporated milk
½ teaspoon salt
Freshly ground pepper to taste
12 chicken drumsticks
¼ cup vegetable oil

Crush the corn chips with a rolling pin, then mix with the cheese. Combine the egg, milk, salt, and pepper in a shallow bowl. Dip the drumsticks first in the milk mixture, then in the crushed chips. Brown on all sides in hot oil in a large, heavy skillet, then lower the heat and simmer, uncovered, for 35 minutes, or until tender. Drain and serve hot. (*Serves 6*)

DEVILED CHICKEN LEGS

8 chicken drumsticks
Salt and freshly ground pepper to taste
Vegetable oil
3 tablespoons butter
¼ teaspoon Worcestershire sauce
1 teaspoon mustard
½ teaspoon crushed dried basil
Fine, dry bread crumbs

Sprinkle the drumsticks with salt and pepper, then brush with oil. Place in a foil-lined baking pan or oven-to-table dish and bake at 350° for 30 minutes, or until the skin is just lightly browned.

Meanwhile, melt the butter in a small saucepan, then stir in the Worcestershire sauce, mustard, and basil. Remove the drumsticks from the oven and brush the butter mixture on. Roll in bread crumbs. Drizzle with any remaining butter. Bake for another 30 minutes, or until the chicken is tender. *(Serves 4)*

BLUE-CHEESED DRUMSTICKS

1 cup sour cream
1 tablespoon lemon juice
1 teaspoon Worcestershire sauce
¼ teaspoon seasoned salt
½ teaspoon paprika
Freshly ground pepper to taste
12 chicken drumsticks
Cracker crumbs
Crumbled blue cheese

Combine the sour cream with the lemon juice, Worcestershire sauce, salt, paprika, and pepper. Dip the chicken in the mixture, then roll in the crumbs. Arrange in a foil-lined baking pan, sprinkle generously with crumbled blue cheese, and bake at 350° for 45 minutes, or until the chicken is tender. *(Serves 6)*

CHICKEN LEGS MARENGO

2 tablespoons vegetable oil
1 clove garlic, peeled
6 whole chicken legs
1 eight-ounce can whole onions, drained
1 twenty-eight-ounce can tomatoes, undrained
1 four-and-one-half-ounce can sliced mushrooms, undrained
2 chicken bouillon cubes
4 sprigs fresh parsley
1 bay leaf
1 teaspoon salt
Freshly ground pepper to taste
¼ teaspoon dried thyme
⅓ cup dry white wine
3 tablespoons all-purpose flour

Heat the oil in a Dutch oven and lightly brown the garlic in it, then discard the garlic. Sauté the chicken legs in the same hot oil until they are uniformly golden brown. Add the onions, tomatoes, mushrooms, bouillon cubes, parsley, bay leaf, salt, pepper, and thyme. Bring to a boil, then reduce the heat and simmer, covered, for 45 minutes, or until the chicken is tender. Stir the wine into the flour to make a paste. Stir the paste into the chicken mixture and bring to a boil, stirring constantly, then reduce the heat and simmer for another 5 minutes. (*Serves 6*)

CHICKEN STANSBURY

½ cup (1 stick) melted butter
1 cup commercially prepared French-fried onions, crumbled
1 teaspoon monosodium glutamate
Pinch of poultry seasoning
10 whole chicken legs
3 or more cups corn flakes, rolled into crumbs
⅓ cup coarsely ground pecans
⅓ cup freshly grated, mixed Parmesan and Romano cheese

Combine the butter with the onions, monosodium glutamate, and poultry seasoning, then brush the chicken legs generously with the mixture. Coat the legs thoroughly with a mixture of the corn flakes, pecans, and cheeses. Place the chicken in a buttered baking pan and bake in a 350° oven for about 50 minutes, basting frequently with the remaining butter-onion mixture. (*Serves 10*)

CHICKEN LEGS TARRAGON

8 whole chicken legs
1½ teaspoons salt
Freshly ground pepper
3½ tablespoons butter
¼ cup lemon juice
2½ teaspoons dried tarragon
2½ teaspoons prepared mustard

Gently pull the skin of the thigh away from the meat, being careful not to pull it off entirely. Sprinkle the flesh with salt and pepper. Cream the butter with the remaining ingredients and place about 2½ teaspoons of the mixture under the skin of each thigh. Wrap the skin around the thighs and secure with bamboo skewers.

Line a broiling pan with foil and place the chicken pieces skin side down. Broil 6 inches from the heat source for about 12 or 15 minutes on one side, or until brown; turn and broil for another 12 or 15 minutes.

To serve, spread any remaining tarragon butter on the chicken, place on a serving platter, and pour the pan juices over. (*Serves 8*)

7 Wings

Winged Victory

The victory belongs to the creative cook who, though tied to a restrictive budget, recognizes that the chicken hides the quintessence of epicurean economy in (if not under) its low-cost wing.

WINGS FISCHER

16 chicken wings
¼ cup vegetable oil
2 bunches green onions, green part and all, cut diagonally
½ pound fresh mushrooms, sliced
¼ cup honey
¼ cup soy sauce
¼ cup water, more if necessary
¼ cup sherry, more if necessary
Thinly slivered peel of ½ orange or tangerine
Hot, cooked rice

Fold the tip of each chicken wing under to form a triangle. Heat the oil in a large frying pan and sauté the wings until golden, then remove to a flat baking dish. In the same oil, brown the onions, then add the mushrooms and cook until *just* limp. Add to the wings. Combine all the other ingredients except the rice and add to the wings as well. (The wings must be covered to three-quarters of their depth. If the liquid does not seem adequate, add enough sherry and water, mixed equally, to make up the difference.)

Cover and bake in a 300° oven for 1 hour, basting and turning the wings at least once, then uncover and baste and turn again while cooking another 25 minutes, by which time the wings should be nicely browned. Serve very hot over the hot, cooked rice. (*Serves 4*)

Note: This is an unusually good dish when accompanied by steamed Chinese snow pea pods and water chestnuts.

CHINESE CHICKEN WINGS

16 chicken wings
3 tablespoons butter
1 small onion, sliced
1 twelve-ounce can pineapple chunks, drained but syrup reserved
Orange juice
¼ cup soy sauce
2 tablespoons brown sugar
1 tablespoon vinegar
1 teaspoon ground ginger
½ teaspoon each salt, ground mace, and Tabasco
¼ teaspoon dry mustard
1½ tablespoons cornstarch
Hot, cooked rice

Fold the tip of each chicken wing under to form a triangle. Melt the butter in a large skillet, add the wings and onion, and cook until the wings are brown on both sides (about 10 minutes). Pour the reserved pineapple syrup into a measuring cup and add enough orange juice to make 1¼ cups liquid, then combine with all the other ingredients except the pineapple chunks, cornstarch, and rice and pour over the chicken.

Cover and simmer for about 30 minutes, or until tender, basting the top pieces with the liquid once or twice. Remove the wings to a hot platter. Thicken the sauce by adding a little cold water to the cornstarch and blending in some of the hot liquid. Add the cornstarch mixture to the hot liquid in the skillet along with the pineapple chunks. Stir slowly and bring to a boil. Serve the wings and sauce over the hot, cooked rice. (*Serves 4*)

JAPANESE CHICKEN WINGS

16 chicken wings
⅔ cup soy sauce
¼ cup dry white wine
1 clove garlic, put through a press
2 tablespoons granulated sugar
1 slice fresh ginger, crushed, or
½ teaspoon ground ginger
¼ cup melted butter

Fold the tip of each chicken wing under to form a triangle, then place the wings in a shallow bowl. Combine the soy sauce, wine, garlic, sugar, and ginger and pour over the wings. Allow to marinate at least 2 or 3 hours, but preferably overnight.

When ready to cook, drain the wings and arrange in a foil-lined broiler pan. Brush with the melted butter and broil for about 25 minutes, turning once, with the wings no closer than 5 inches to the heat source. (*Serves 4*)

SWEET AND SOUR WINGS

12 chicken wings
1 tablespoon ground ginger
3/4 cup all-purpose flour
1/2 cup vegetable oil
1 cup pineapple chunks, drained but syrup reserved
1/2 cup each vinegar and soy sauce
1 tablespoon Worcestershire sauce
3/4 cup granulated sugar
Salt and freshly ground pepper to taste
1 green pepper, sliced
1 1/2 cups canned, drained bean sprouts
1 eight-ounce can water chestnuts, thinly sliced
2 tomatoes, quartered
2 tablespoons chili sauce
Hot, cooked rice

Fold the tip of each wing under to form a triangle. Combine the ginger and half the flour in a paper bag. Place the wings, a couple at a time, in the bag and shake to coat, then brown on all sides in the hot oil, removing them to a platter as they finish browning.

Add enough water to the reserved pineapple syrup to measure 1 3/4 cups. Gradually stir in the remaining flour, then stir this mixture, along with the vinegar, soy sauce, and Worcestershire sauce into the pan drippings. Heat to boiling, stirring constantly, and boil for 1 minute, then add the sugar, salt, pepper, and wings.

Cover and simmer for 30 minutes, stirring occasionally, then add the pineapple and green pepper and cook for 5 minutes, uncovered. Stir in the bean sprouts, water chestnuts, tomatoes, and chili sauce and cook for 5 minutes longer. Serve over the rice. (*Serves 4 to 6*)

CHILI WINGS

16 chicken wings
1 egg, well beaten with 1 tablespoon water
2 cups dehydrated potato flakes
Salt to taste
2 teaspoons chili powder
¼ cup melted butter

Fold the tip of each wing under to form a triangle. Dip into the egg-water combination, then into the potato flakes blended with the salt and chili powder. Place in a shallow, well-buttered baking pan, drizzle lightly with melted butter, and bake in a 350° oven for about 40 minutes, or until nicely browned and tender. (*Serves 4*)

WINGS, YAMS, AND PINEAPPLE

16 chicken wings
¾ cup all-purpose flour
1 teaspoon salt
Freshly ground pepper
½ cup evaporated milk
¼ cup (½ stick) butter
1 twenty-nine-ounce can yams, drained
1 one-pound can pineapple chunks, drained but syrup reserved
1 teaspoon soy sauce
3 tablespoons brown sugar

Fold the tip of each chicken wing under to form a triangle. Combine the flour with the salt and pepper and place in a paper bag. Dip the wings in evaporated milk, then shake with the flour in the bag to coat.

Melt the butter in a baking dish in a 425° oven. Arrange

the wings in the pan and brown on each side (about 15 minutes per side), then remove the pan from the oven and arrange the yams and pineapple chunks between the wings. Combine the reserved syrup with the soy sauce and brown sugar and spoon over all. Return to the oven and bake for 20 minutes, or until heated through. (*Serves 4 to 6*)

BROILER-BARBECUED WINGS

- **16 chicken wings**
- **2 tablespoons Dijon mustard**
- **¼ cup cider vinegar**
- **¾ cup catsup**
- **½ cup molasses**
- **2 tablespoons vegetable oil**
- **2 teaspoons Worcestershire sauce**
- **½ teaspoon salt**
- **¼ teaspoon garlic powder**
- **¼ teaspoon Louisiana hot sauce**

Preheat the broiler. Fold the tip of each chicken wing under to form a triangle, then arrange the wings on the broiler pan. Combine the remaining ingredients and brush liberally on the wings, then broil, 6 inches from the heat source, for 30 to 40 minutes, turning frequently and basting until the sauce is used up. (*Serves 4*)

FRUIT-BRAISED WINGS

- **16 chicken wings**
- **2 tablespoons butter**
- **1 twenty-ounce can sliced pie apples**
- **1 cup dry white wine**
- **Salt and freshly ground pepper to taste**

Fold the tip of each chicken wing under to form a triangle, then brown the wings in hot, bubbling butter in a frying pan. Remove the wings to a heatproof casserole and arrange them in a single layer. Place the apple slices over the wings.

Pour the wine into the frying pan and swirl it about with a wooden spoon, making sure you get up all the nice browned bits. Pour the wine over the wings, season with salt and pepper, then cover the casserole tightly and bake in a 350° oven for about 45 minutes, or until the wings are fork tender. (*Serves 4 to 6*)

WINGS MIDAS

16 chicken wings
¼ cup all-purpose flour
Salt to taste
1 teaspoon paprika
¼ cup (½ stick) butter
2½ teaspoons curry powder
1 ten-and-one-half-ounce can condensed cream of chicken soup, undiluted
1 cup water
1 one-pound can peach slices, drained
Slivered, toasted almonds

Fold the tip of each wing under to form a triangle. Shake in a bag with the flour, salt, and paprika, then sauté in hot butter until golden all over. Sprinkle with curry powder, then stir in the soup and water and simmer, covered, for about 40 minutes, or until fork tender. Add the peaches and heat through for 5 minutes. Sprinkle with the almonds and serve with hot, steamed rice. (*Serves 4 to 6*)

BAKED WINGS

- 16 chicken wings
- ¾ cup tomato juice
- 2 cups water
- Salt and freshly ground pepper to taste
- ¼ teaspoon granulated sugar
- ½ cup chopped onion
- 1 clove garlic, put through a press
- All-purpose flour
- Chicken broth (optional)

Fold the tip of each wing under to form a triangle, then place in a roasting pan with all the other ingredients except the flour and optional chicken broth. Stir well, then cover and bake at 375° for 40 minutes, or until tender. Remove the wings to a hot platter and thicken the pan drippings with flour, adding chicken broth, if necessary. Serve with steamed rice, noodles, or mashed potatoes. (*Serves 4 to 6*)

SKILLET-GLAZED WINGS

- 16 chicken wings
- 2 tablespoons butter
- ½ cup water
- 2 tablespoons ginger marmalade
- ½ teaspoon salt
- Freshly ground pepper

Tuck the tip of each wing under to form a triangle, then brown in hot, melted butter. Add the water, marmalade, salt, and pepper. Cover and simmer for about 45 minutes, or until fork tender, turning and basting with the sauce frequently to form a glaze. (*Serves 4*)

WINGS STROGANOFF

16 chicken wings
¼ cup (½ stick) butter
2 ten-and-one-half-ounce cans steak-and-mushroom sauce
1 cup dry white wine
Salt and freshly ground pepper to taste
1 cup sour cream

Tuck the tip of each wing under to form a triangle, then brown lightly in hot butter in a large, deepish skillet. Add the sauce, then rinse out the cans with the wine and add it to the wings. Season with salt and pepper, then cover and cook gently for about 40 minutes, or until the wings are fork tender. Carefully blend in the sour cream and cook only until it is heated through. Serve with noodles. (*Serves 4 to 6*)

BATTERED WINGS

Chicken Wings

16 chicken wings
2 tablespoons butter
1 teaspoon salt
1 teaspoon curry powder
1 cup chicken broth
Fat for deep frying

Batter

Milk
1 whole egg, beaten
1⅓ cups sifted all-purpose flour
½ teaspoon salt
1½ teaspoons baking powder

Sauce

½ cup catsup
¼ cup hot mustard

Tuck the tip of each wing under to form a triangle, then place in a baking dish. Dot with the butter, season with salt and curry powder, and pour in the broth. Cover and bake in a 350° oven for about 40 minutes, or until tender.

When the 40 minutes are up, remove the chicken from the oven and make the batter.

Pour the chicken drippings from the baking pan into a cup and add enough milk to make ⅔ cup of liquid. Add to the beaten egg. Sift the flour, salt, and baking powder directly into the egg and milk mixture and beat with a whisk until very smooth. Dip the chicken in the batter and fry, 4 wings at a time, in deep hot fat (365°) until golden brown. Drain on absorbent paper and serve as hot as possible, accompanied by a sauce made by combining and heating the catsup and mustard. (*Serves 4*)

BRAISED WINGS

16 chicken wings
1 small onion, chopped
⅓ cup butter
Salt and freshly ground pepper to taste
⅔ cup sherry

Fold the tip of each wing under to form a triangle. Cook the onion until limp in very hot butter, then remove from the pan and set aside. Brown the chicken wings on both sides in the same pan, then return the onions to the pan and add the salt, pepper, and wine. Cover and simmer about 40 minutes, or until the wings are fork tender. Serve with noodles. (*Serves 4*)

SAVORY WINGS

- **16 chicken wings**
- **2 tablespoons butter**
- **¾ cup chopped celery**
- **¾ cup chopped onion**
- **1 cup catsup**
- **1½ tablespoons cider vinegar**
- **2 teaspoons Worcestershire sauce**
- **2 teaspoons Dijon mustard**
- **¾ cup water**
- **Salt and freshly ground pepper to taste**

Tuck the tip of each wing under to form a triangle, then brown lightly in hot butter in a skillet. Remove to a baking dish. Add the celery and onion to the pan drippings and cook until tender. Add the remaining ingredients, bring to a boil, and pour over the wings. Bake, uncovered, in a 375° oven for 40 to 45 minutes, or until the wings are fork tender, basting several times. Serve with noodles. (*Serves 4 to 6*)

8 Livers

Chicken livers have always sounded very elegant to me. I don't know why. My reaction may be triggered by some half-remembered childhood experience, but whatever—chicken livers *taste* very elegant, and there's little more one can ask of any food.

Other recipes for chicken livers will be found in the chapter on Appetizers, page 6–14.

CHICKEN LIVER OMELET

½ pound chicken livers
Salt and freshly ground pepper to taste
Pinch of ground cinnamon
Pinch of ground mace
1 tablespoon all-purpose flour
1 tablespoon butter
1 tablespoon sherry
1 four-egg omelet

Season the chicken livers with the salt, pepper, cinnamon, and mace, then dredge with the flour and sauté in the butter over low heat until very lightly browned. Just before removing, stir in the sherry until mixture thickens, but does not boil. Fold into a four-egg omelet cooked your favorite way (or even simple scrambled eggs) and serve at once. (*Serves 2 to 3*)

CHICKEN LIVERS À LA RUSSE

- **¼ cup (½ stick) butter**
- **1 pound chicken livers, halved**
- **1 small onion, minced**
- **2½ teaspoons arrowroot**
- **1 four-ounce can mushrooms, chopped**
- **¾ cup chicken stock**
- **1 cup sour cream**
- **1 teaspoon Spice Islands Beau Monde seasoning**
- **Salt and freshly ground pepper to taste**
- **2 tablespoons sherry**
- **1 tablespoon minced fresh parsley**

Heat the butter in a skillet and brown the livers for 5 minutes, turning frequently. Remove the livers, then add the onion, arrowroot, mushrooms, and stock to the skillet and cook, stirring, until thickened. Stir in the sour cream and seasonings. Return the livers to pan, add the sherry, and stir well. Heat through, but do not boil. Sprinkle with the parsley and serve with noodles or rice. (*Serves 4 to 6*)

SPAGHETTI WITH CHICKEN LIVERS

- **2½ cups fresh-stewed or canned tomatoes**
- **1 clove garlic, put through a press**
- **1 onion, chopped**
- **2 teaspoons celery salt**
- **½ teaspoon ground ginger**
- **Salt and freshly ground pepper to taste**
- **1 teaspoon granulated sugar**
- **Dash of cayenne**
- **1 cup beef stock or 1 beef bouillon cube dissolved in 1 cup boiling water**

½ pound chicken livers, chopped coarsely
1 cup sliced mushrooms
¼ cup (½ stick) butter
2 tablespoons all-purpose flour
½ pound spaghetti or vermicelli
½ cup freshly grated Parmesan cheese

Combine the tomatoes, garlic, onion, celery salt, ginger, salt, pepper, sugar, and cayenne in a saucepan. Cook together slowly for about 30 minutes, then add the stock. In a separate pan, sauté the livers and mushrooms in hot butter until tender. Add the flour and the tomato mixture, blending well; then cook gently for 15 minutes.

Meanwhile, cook the spaghetti, following package directions, and drain. Add the sauce to the spaghetti, tossing lightly. Sprinkle with the cheese and serve. (*Serves 6*)

CHICKEN LIVERS EN BROCHETTE

1 pound chicken livers, halved
Juice of 1 lemon
24 small mushrooms
12 strips bacon, halved
12 water chestnuts
¼ cup (½ stick) butter
Minced fresh parsley
Well-buttered toast

Dip the chicken liver halves in the lemon juice and blot dry with paper toweling. Snap the stems off the mushrooms and save for another day (they're fine chopped), then wipe the mushroom caps with a damp cloth or towel. Thread 3 chicken livers, 2 pieces bacon, 2 mushroom caps and 1 water chestnut alternately on each of 12 ten-inch skewers. Brush with the butter blended with the chopped parsley and broil about

6 inches from the heat source until very lightly browned. Turn, brush with more parsleyed butter, and broil for another 6 minutes.

Serve 2 kebabs per person, placing them on the well-buttered toast. (*Serves 6*)

Note: These may also be cooked on the barbecue grill.

LEMON-BUTTERED LIVERS

1 pound chicken livers
All-purpose flour
¼ cup (½ stick) butter
Salt and freshly ground pepper to taste
2 tablespoons lemon juice
2 tablespoons chopped fresh parsley
Toast points

Dredge the livers in the flour, then cook in melted butter until lightly browned on all sides. Remove livers from the pan, sprinkle with salt and pepper, and set aside to keep warm.

Heat the butter remaining in the pan until it becomes a light brown, then pour over the livers. Sprinkle the livers with lemon juice and chopped parsley, and serve on toast points. (*Serves 4*)

SAUTÉED CHICKEN LIVERS

1 pound chicken livers, halved
½ pound mushrooms, sliced
3 tablespoons butter
Salt and freshly ground pepper to taste
¼ teaspoon dried thyme
½ cup dry white wine
Minced fresh parsley for garnish

Sauté the chicken livers and mushrooms in melted butter until lightly browned and the mushroom liquid has cooked away; do not overcook the livers. Add the seasonings and wine and cook rapidly, uncovered, until the wine has almost evaporated. Sprinkle with parsley and serve. (*Serves 4 to 6*)

CHICKEN LIVERS MADEIRA

8 slices bacon, diced
1 small onion, chopped
2 cloves garlic, put through a press
2 pounds chicken livers
¾ cup all-purpose flour
2 four-ounce cans mushrooms
¼ cup (½ stick) butter
Salt and freshly ground pepper to taste
⅛ teaspoon dried thyme
2 ten-and-one-half-ounce cans condensed beef broth (bouillon), undiluted
⅓ cup Madeira or sherry
¼ cup chopped fresh parsley
Hot, cooked rice

Cook the bacon until crisp, then remove from the skillet. Drain all but 3 tablespoons bacon fat from the skillet and cook the onion and garlic. Dredge the livers in ½ cup of the flour and add to the skillet, along with the drained mushrooms. Cook, adding more fat, if necessary, until the livers are just tender (about 6 to 8 minutes).

In a separate saucepan, melt the butter and stir in the remaining flour, the salt, pepper, and thyme and cook until smooth. Gradually stir in the broth, then cook and stir until thick and smooth. Stir in the wine. Add the liver mixture, bacon, and parsley and heat through. Serve over a bed of hot rice. (*Serves 6 to 8*)

CHICKEN LIVERS SAUTERNE

- **8 slices bacon, diced**
- **4 green onions, sliced**
- **1 four-and-one-half-ounce can sliced mushrooms, drained**
- **Pinch of rosemary**
- **1½ pounds chicken livers**
- **½ cup dry Sauterne**
- **½ cup chicken broth**
- **1 chicken bouillon cube**
- **Steamed rice**

Brown the bacon lightly in a skillet, then add the onions, mushrooms, and rosemary. Sauté for 1 minute, or until the onions are soft, then add the livers and sauté for 5 minutes. Add the wine, broth, and bouillon cube and simmer for 2 or 3 minutes. Serve over steamed rice. (*Serves 6*)

QUICK CHICK LIVERS

- **1 pound chicken livers**
- **1 envelope seasoned coating mix for chicken**
- **Toast points, rice, or noodles**

Coat the livers with the mix and place on a foil-lined baking sheet. Bake in a 425° oven for 12 to 15 minutes, then serve on toast points, rice or noodles. (*Serves 4*)

CHICKEN LIVERS POLYNESIAN

¼ cup (½ stick) butter
¼ cup slivered green pepper
½ cup chopped onion
1 cup diagonally cut celery
1½ pounds chicken livers
¼ cup brown sugar, packed
¼ cup granulated sugar
¼ cup cornstarch
1 cup pineapple juice
5 tablespoons cider vinegar
1 tablespoon soy sauce
2 cups chopped fresh pineapple
2 pineapple half shells
½ cup slivered almonds

Melt the butter in a frying pan. Add the green pepper, onion, and celery and cook for 5 minutes, then add the livers and cook another 10 minutes, stirring frequently.

In a small saucepan combine the sugars, cornstarch, pineapple juice, vinegar, and soy sauce. Bring to a boil and cook, stirring constantly, until thickened. Add the sauce and pineapple to the liver mixture and serve in the pineapple shells, garnished with the almonds. Chinese noodles are a perfect accompaniment. (*Serves 4 to 6*)

FRENCH-FRIED CHICKEN LIVERS

2½ cups boiling water, approximately
Juice and grated rind of ½ lemon
1 pound chicken livers
1½ cups soy sauce
½ teaspoon ground cinnamon

6 tablespoons granulated sugar
Oil for deep frying
3 green onions, minced
¼ cup slivered, toasted almonds

Pour the lemon juice into the boiling water, then add the rind. Add the livers and adjust the water level, as the water should *just* cover them. Cover the pot and allow to come to a boil. Remove from the heat, let stand for 5 minutes, then drain. Rinse the livers in cold water and drain again.

In a small saucepan, combine the soy sauce, cinnamon, and sugar. Add the livers and heat slowly. Let simmer for 10 minutes, without boiling, then drain.

Heat oil for deep frying in a deep fryer or very deep skillet. Fry the livers quickly, as they should be nice and crusty outside, but soft inside, and serve at once, sprinkled with chopped green onions and slivered almonds. (*Serves 4*)

CHICKEN LIVERS IN SOUR CREAM

3 tablespoons butter
1 pound chicken livers, halved
1 small onion, finely chopped
Salt and freshly ground pepper to taste
1 cup sour cream
Hot, cooked rice or buckwheat groats

Heat the butter in a large skillet and cook the livers and onion, seasoning with salt and pepper to taste, until the livers no longer run pink when pierced with a fork; do not overcook. Pour in the sour cream, blend, and cook just long enough to heat through. Serve over rice or buckwheat groats. (*Serves 4*)

CHICKEN LIVERS WITH MUSHROOMS

½ pound mushrooms, sliced
1 pound chicken livers, halved
¼ cup (½ stick) butter
¾ teaspoon dried rosemary
Salt and freshly ground pepper to taste
Minced fresh parsley
¼ cup dry red wine
Toast points

Sauté the mushrooms and chicken livers in melted butter until lightly browned (about 6 to 8 minutes). Add the rosemary, salt, pepper, 2 tablespoons minced parsley, and wine and simmer, uncovered, until the wine is almost absorbed. Garnish with additional parsley and serve on toast points. (*Serves 4*)

9 Fried and Sautéed

Frying Pan, Skillet, or Spider

Fried chicken may well be America's all-time sweetheart, but there's more than one way to fry it. Every cook across the land has his or her own favorite, regional, hand-me-down "receipt," so I'll just offer a few of my own standbys and then go on to prove that a frying pan (by any other name) isn't necessarily just for frying, after all.

CHICKEN MARYLAND

1 three-and-one-half-pound fryer, disjointed
¼ cup all-purpose flour
¾ teaspoon salt
Freshly ground pepper to taste
¼ teaspoon paprika
1 egg, beaten with 2 tablespoons water
Fresh, soft bread crumbs
½ cup (1 stick) butter

Shake the chicken parts in a paper bag with the flour and seasonings. Dip the pieces in the egg-water mixture, then into the bread crumbs. Lay the pieces out on waxed paper to dry for about 1 hour, then heat the butter to sizzling in a large, heavy frying pan, add the chicken, and brown it well on all sides. Lower the heat and cook the chicken gently for about 30 to 40 minutes, or until it is fork tender. Serve with your favorite old-fashioned cream gravy. (*Serves 4*)

FRIED CHICKEN WITH SOUR CREAM GRAVY

1 three-pound fryer, disjointed
¼ cup (½ stick) butter
Salt and freshly ground pepper to taste
¼ teaspoon dried oregano
¼ cup water
½ cup sherry
⅔ cup sour cream

Brown the chicken parts in hot, bubbly butter. When they are browned on all sides, sprinkle with salt, pepper, and oregano. Combine the water and sherry and pour over the chicken, then cover the frying pan and cook gently for about 30 minutes, or until the chicken is fork tender. Remove the chicken to a hot platter and keep warm.

Stir up the juices in the pan, then remove from fire and carefully add the sour cream. Return the chicken to the pan, reheat for a few moments, then serve, smothered in gravy. (*Serves 4*)

Note: Homemade biscuits go well with this.

FRIED CHICKEN WITH PEANUT CRUST

1 whole egg
1 cup plus 2 tablespoons whole milk
½ cup cracker crumbs
⅔ cup ground, salted peanuts
Salt and pepper to taste
1 three-pound fryer, disjointed
¼ cup (½ stick) butter
2 tablespoons all-purpose flour

Beat the egg with the 2 tablespoons milk; combine the crumbs and ground peanuts with salt and pepper to taste. Dip the chicken pieces in the egg-milk mixture, then in the crumb-peanut mixture. Brown in hot, bubbly butter, then lower the heat and cook until the chicken is tender (about 40 minutes). Drain the chicken pieces on crumpled paper towels.

Remove all but 2 tablespoons fat from the frying pan, but leave in all the delicious, browned bits from the chicken (it won't make a smooth gravy, but it will be unusually tasty). Blend the flour into the pan drippings, stirring until smooth, then slowly blend in the cup of milk. When the gravy has thickened, adjust the seasoning. Return the chicken to the pan to reheat, and serve at once with a big bowl of fluffy mashed potatoes. (*Serves 4 to 6*)

BEER-BATTERED CHICKEN

1 cup sifted all-purpose flour
Salt and freshly ground pepper to taste
1 teaspoon paprika
2 eggs, separated
⅔ cup beer
2 tablespoons melted butter
1 three-and-one-half-pound fryer, disjointed
Fat for deep frying

Resift the flour with the seasonings. Beat the egg yolks until light, then add the beer and stir the mixture into the flour until *just* blended. Stir in the melted butter and allow the batter to rest at room temperature until light and frothy (about 1½ hours), then beat the egg whites until stiff, and fold into the batter. Dip the chicken pieces, one by one, into the batter and place on a cookie sheet. Refrigerate for about 1 hour.

Remove the chicken from the refrigerator 15 minutes before you wish to fry it, then fry to a golden brown in deep fat at 360°. Place the fried chicken pieces on a cookie sheet and bake in a 350° oven for about 40 minutes, or until fork tender. (*Serves 4 to 6*)

FRYING PAN BARBECUE

1 three-pound fryer, disjointed
¼ cup all-purpose flour
Salt and freshly ground pepper to taste
¾ teaspoon paprika
½ cup shortening
¼ cup chopped onion
½ cup chopped green pepper
2 eight-ounce cans tomato sauce
3 tablespoons granulated sugar
3 tablespoons wine vinegar
1½ teaspoons Worcestershire sauce
Dash of Tabasco

Roll the chicken pieces in the flour mixed with salt, pepper, and paprika. Heat the shortening in a frying pan and cook the onion and green pepper until soft and golden in color, then remove the vegetables and set aside. Fry the chicken in the remaining fat until nicely browned on all sides, then lower the heat and cook another 35 to 40 minutes, or until tender. Remove the chicken and pour off the fat.

Place the vegetables and the remaining ingredients in the pan, blend well, and simmer for 5 minutes. Return the chicken to the sauce and cook another 10 minutes, making sure each piece is nicely coated with the sauce. (*Serves 4 to 6*)

HOBO CHICKEN

2 teaspoons salt
1 teaspoon monosodium glutamate
½ teaspoon cracked or coarsely ground pepper
1 teaspoon paprika
1 teaspoon mixed herb seasoning
1 three-pound fryer, disjointed
¼ cup (½ stick) butter
¼ cup minced onion
1 tablespoon sesame seeds

Combine the salt, monosodium glutamate, pepper, paprika, and herb seasoning and rub the chicken pieces with the mixture. Fry the chicken in hot, bubbling butter until well-browned. Turn and sprinkle with the minced onion and sesame seeds, then lower the heat and continue cooking until the chicken is tender (about 40 minutes). *(Serves 4 to 6)*

Here we jump from the frying pan into the sauté pan, which to all intents and purposes are one and the same. Only the method is different.

SIMPLE SAUTÉED CHICKEN

1 three-pound fryer, quartered
¼ cup (½ stick) butter
1 cup sliced mushrooms
2 cups light cream or half-and-half
⅔ cup Benedictine

Sauté the chicken slowly in hot butter, with the cover on the pan, turning occasionally. When the chicken is golden and tender (about 40 minutes), add the mushrooms and cream. Stir well and bring *just* to a boil. Immediately before serving, add the Benedictine and stir quickly. (*Serves 4*)

APPLED CHICKEN

2 two-pound fryers, disjointed
½ cup (1 stick) sweet butter
6 tablespoons brandy, warmed
6 to 8 green onions, white part only, minced
1 tablespoon minced fresh parsley
1 tablespoon dried thyme
Salt and freshly ground pepper to taste
¾ cup apple wine or ½ cup apple cider
½ cup evaporated milk, undiluted, or ½ cup heavy cream

Sauté the chicken pieces in the butter until about half done, then pour the brandy over the chicken and flame it (using a long fireplace match for safety's sake). Add the minced onion, parsley, thyme, salt, and pepper, blend well, and add the apple wine or cider. Cover and cook on low heat until the chicken is fork tender (about 30 minutes). Just before serving, add the evaporated milk or the cream, stirring well into the pan juices. Correct the seasoning and serve very hot. (*Serves 4 to 6*)

CHERRIED CHICKEN

- **1 twelve-ounce jar cherry preserves**
- **1 tablespoon vinegar**
- **5 whole cloves**
- **Salt**
- **¼ teaspoon ground allspice**
- **¼ teaspoon ground mace**
- **1 three-pound fryer, quartered**
- **⅓ cup butter**
- **Freshly ground pepper**

Combine the preserves, vinegar, cloves, 1 teaspoon salt, the allspice, and mace in a small saucepan. Mix well, heat slowly, and cook for about 10 minutes. Keep warm.

In a large skillet, brown the chicken on all sides in the butter, adding salt and pepper to taste. Cover and cook gently until almost tender (about 40 minutes), then drain off the fat. Pour half the cherry sauce over the chicken, cover, and finish cooking.

When done, arrange the chicken in a serving dish and cover with the remaining sauce. (*Serves 4*)

CHICKEN FOR THE BOSS'S WIFE

- **½ cup (1 stick) butter**
- **3 tablespoons salad oil**
- **1 four-pound chicken, disjointed**
- **24 shallots, peeled**
- **Salt and freshly ground pepper to taste**
- **1 ten-ounce package frozen artichoke hearts, cooked**

Melt half the butter in a large, heavy frying pan, then add the salad oil. Brown the chicken pieces in the mixture, removing them as they get browned to a hot platter. Add the shallots to the pan and cook until they are golden, stirring occasionally. Pour off some of the fat, then return the chicken to the pan. Season with salt and pepper to taste and quickly bring to a boil, then turn down the heat at once and cook another 10 minutes, basting all the while with the pan juices. Cover and allow to cook gently for 20 minutes, or until fork tender.

Meanwhile, melt the remaining butter in a small frying pan and sauté the artichokes until they turn a light gold. Place the chicken in the center of a large platter and surround it with shallots and artichokes. Pour the remaining pan juices over the chicken just before serving. (*Serves 4 to 6*)

COCONUT CHICKEN SAUTÉ

1 three-and-one-half-pound fryer, disjointed
3 tablespoons butter
½ cup sour cream
¼ cup prepared mustard (I like Dijon)
¼ cup milk
½ cup flaked coconut

Brown the chicken parts in the butter. Pour off the excess fat, then cover and cook over low heat for 35 to 40 minutes, or until tender, turning occasionally. Blend together the sour cream, mustard, and milk. Pour over the chicken and cook, uncovered, for another 5 minutes (do not boil). Then sprinkle with the coconut and serve. (*Serves 4*)

CHICKEN SAUTÉ JOHANNA

3 tablespoons butter
1 three-and-one-half-pound fryer, quartered
Salt and freshly ground pepper to taste
1 small onion, chopped
½ carrot, sliced
½ cup dry white wine
1 cup heavy cream
3 tablespoons brandy

Heat the butter in a large frying pan and add the chicken quarters, salt, pepper, onion, and carrot. Cover and allow the chicken to cook without browning. In 30 minutes, or when the bird is almost but not quite done, discard the carrot slices, then allow the chicken to finish cooking. When the chicken is done, remove it and keep it hot in a deep serving dish. Stir in the white wine and allow it to cook down, then add the cream and simmer for a few minutes. Add the brandy and heat, stirring. Pour the sauce over the chicken and serve. (*Serves 4*)

SPICY CHICKEN SAUTÉ

3 tablespoons butter
1 three-pound fryer, disjointed
¼ teaspoon ground ginger
½ teaspoon turmeric
6 whole cloves
1 one-inch piece cinnamon stick, broken up
¼ teaspoon ground cardamom
2 small onions, sliced thin
½ clove garlic, put through a press
¼ teaspoon chili powder
1 teaspoon salt

Melt the butter in a heavy frying pan and add the chicken. Sprinkle with the ginger, turmeric, cloves, broken-up cinnamon stick, and cardamom and brown on all sides. When chicken is well browned, top with the onion rings, garlic, chili powder, and salt. Cover the pan and cook very slowly for about 30 minutes. Shake the frying pan every 8 to 10 minutes, but do not remove the lid. After 30 to 35 minutes, test for doneness and adjust the seasoning. (*Serves 4*)

CHICKEN SAUTÉ PARISIENNE

1 four-pound fryer, disjointed
Salt and freshly ground pepper to taste
¼ cup (½ stick) butter
3 tablespoons brandy
4 shallots, chopped
1 cup champagne
1 tomato, peeled and chopped
¾ teaspoon paprika
½ teaspoon dried tarragon
1 egg yolk
¼ cup heavy cream

Rub the chicken parts thoroughly with generous amounts of salt and pepper. Melt the butter in a heavy skillet and brown the chicken in it. Add the brandy, stirring to blend with the pan juices, then add the shallots, champagne, tomato, paprika, and tarragon. Cover and cook very gently for 40 to 45 minutes, or until the chicken is tender.

When the chicken is done, beat the egg yolk and the cream together in a bowl. Pour most of the sauce from the chicken into this mixture, pouring slowly and beating constantly to prevent curdling. Reheat, but do not allow to boil. Arrange the chicken on a platter and pour the sauce over it. (*Serves 6*)

10 Roast Chicken

Stuffed Every Which Way

Traditional roast chicken is a basic blessing. Easy to prepare, beautiful to serve, delicious to eat, its taste and texture differ tantalizingly according to which of an infinite variety of stuffings you choose.

BASIC ROAST CHICKEN

Select a broiler-fryer, roaster, or capon weighing a minimum of 3 to 3½ pounds. Be sure the fowl is at room temperature before working with it.

Wash the chicken, inside and out, then pat dry with paper toweling. (Instead of washing the bird, I like to rub it inside and out with a cut lemon.)

Gently simmer the neck, heart, giblets, and liver until tender with salt and pepper to taste, a rib of celery, an onion, and a good-sized bay leaf. This aromatic liquid becomes the basis for gravy, or even better if you're weight-watching, it can be strained and frozen as part of your hoard of indispensable chicken stock (see also page 16).

Your stuffing may be prepared a day ahead and refrigerated. But *under no circumstances* stuff the bird itself until you are ready to put it into the oven. Stuff the neck cavity lightly (the dressing swells considerably in the cooking), then pull the skin of the neck across the opening to the back and skewer it neatly. Turn the wings up and back so the wing tips rest against the neck skin; this makes a level bed on which the bird can rest. Stuff the body cavity lightly and truss the opening with poultry pins laced with white string. The string should be long enough to wrap around the leg ends and tail so they can be drawn in close to the body.

Lay the stuffed, trussed bird on a rack in a shallow roasting pan. Dip a double thickness of cheesecloth in melted butter and drape it over the top and sides of the chicken. Don't let the cloth dry out; baste it from time to time with natural pan juices and a little more melted butter.

Roast the chicken, uncovered, in a 375° oven until the legs move easily in their sockets. (For goodness' sake, don't pierce the flesh with a fork—you'll lose that marvelous juice!) To roast, figure 30 minutes to the pound. Undrape the chicken during the last 45 minutes of cooking so that it browns nicely. At this time, too, you can give the bird a very elegant look by glazing it (see page 106).

Two cups of dressing will stuff a 4-pound bird nicely. If you have a superabundance of dressing, it can be baked in a covered casserole for an hour, along with the chicken.

DHU'S SUPER SOUFFLÉ STUFFING

The amounts given here will stuff 2 six-pound birds. You will need this amount, as the demand always exceeds the supply.

1 cup (2 sticks) butter
1 large loaf soft white bread, crusts removed and reserved for another purpose
8 green onions, green part and all, chopped fine

½ cup minced fresh parsley
Salt and freshly ground pepper to taste
1 dozen eggs

Melt the butter in a large saucepan over low heat. Pull the doughy part of the bread into smallish pieces and add to the melted butter. Mix in the chopped onion, parsley, salt, and pepper, then break the eggs directly into the concoction and stir well. (Don't worry if the stuffing looks soupy—it's supposed to.) Fill the neck and body cavities lightly—*very* lightly, as this stuffing puffs and rises like a true soufflé. And I hope you make enough!

ROSE'S FARFEL STUFFING

1 12-ounce box "bake type" farfel (a barley-sized kosher egg noodle)
Boiling salted water
2 large onions, chopped
½ cup (1 stick) butter
½ pound mushrooms, sliced
Salt and freshly ground pepper to taste

Boil the farfel, following package directions, until tender. Meanwhile, sauté the onion and mushrooms in the butter. Drain the farfel thoroughly in a colander, then mix farfel with sautéed onions and mushrooms. Season to taste and mix well. (*Enough for 2 four-pound birds*)

ALMOND STUFFING

- ½ cup (1 stick) butter
- Liver from a 6-pound chicken, chopped
- ½ cup minced onion
- ½ cup finely chopped celery
- ½ cup chopped, unblanched almonds
- 3 cups toasted white bread cubes
- ½ teaspoon salt
- ½ teaspoon dried sage leaves
- ¼ teaspoon nutmeg
- A few grindings of pepper
- 2 tablespoons chopped fresh parsley

Melt the butter in a skillet and sauté the liver, onion, celery, and almonds for 5 minutes, stirring constantly. Toss the mixture in a large bowl with the bread cubes and seasonings, mixing well. (*Enough for 1 six-pound bird*)

WALNUT-RICE STUFFING

- 1 onion, chopped fine
- 1 carrot, grated
- 1 cup finely diced celery
- ¼ cup minced fresh parsley
- ½ cup (1 stick) butter
- 3 cups soft bread crumbs
- Salt and freshly ground pepper to taste
- ¼ teaspoon poultry seasoning
- ¼ teaspoon dried thyme
- 3 cups cooked brown rice
- ½ cup chopped walnuts
- 6 tablespoons chicken broth

Sauté the onion, carrot, celery, and parsley in the butter until soft but not colored. Combine the bread crumbs with the seasonings, then add the sautéed vegetables and toss until well blended. Add the rice, walnuts, and broth, mixing lightly. (*Enough for 1 six-pound bird, plus a small casserole*)

SAUTERNE-RICE STUFFING

¼ cup currants
3 tablespoons butter
1 clove garlic, halved
¾ cup Sauterne
1½ cups water
1 cup raw rice
1 teaspoon salt
Freshly ground pepper to taste
⅛ teaspoon freshly grated nutmeg
⅛ teaspoon ground allspice
1 teaspoon granulated sugar
⅓ cup chopped Brazil nuts

Put the currants in a small saucepan and add enough water to cover. Bring to a boil and remove from the heat. Allow to stand for 5 minutes, then drain.

Melt the butter in a skillet and add the halved garlic. Cook for 5 minutes, then remove and discard the garlic. Add the wine and water to the skillet. Bring to a boil, then stir in the rice, salt, pepper, nutmeg, allspice, and sugar. Bring to a boil again, cover tightly, and cook over very low heat for 25 minutes, or until the rice has absorbed all the liquid. Stir in the currants and nuts. (*Enough for 1 six-pound bird*)

WILD RICE STUFFING

Giblets from a 6-pound chicken
1 cup raw wild rice
¼ cup olive oil
½ cup chopped celery
½ cup chopped onion
¼ cup chopped mushrooms
¼ cup minced green pepper
Chicken broth
1 teaspoon salt
¼ teaspoon dried sage
¼ teaspoon Worcestershire sauce
¼ teaspoon catsup
⅛ teaspoon pepper

Cover the giblets with water and cook until tender. Drain the giblets, reserving the liquid, then chop fine. Wash and drain the rice. Heat the oil in a large skillet and add the giblets, rice, celery, onion, mushrooms, and green pepper. Cook, stirring, until the rice is golden. Add enough chicken broth to the reserved giblet cooking liquid to make 1 cup. Add, along with the remaining ingredients, to the skillet. Cover and simmer for 25 minutes. (*Enough to stuff 1 six-pound bird*)

STUFFING WITH PÂTÉ

5 slices day-old bread, crumbled
¼ cup chopped onion
¼ cup chopped celery leaves
3 tablespoons chopped fresh parsley
Heaping ½ tablespoon dried tarragon, rubbed between the fingers

Salt and freshly ground pepper to taste
1 tablespoon melted butter
1 2¾-ounce can pâté de foie gras

Combine all the ingredients and mix well. (*Enough to stuff 1 six-pound bird*)

ITALIAN STUFFING

1 cup freshly grated, mixed Romano and Parmesan cheese
1 egg
1 sprig parsley, minced
1 clove garlic, put through a press
½ pound pork, cooked and diced
½ teaspoon salt
¼ teaspoon freshly ground pepper

Combine all the ingredients and mix well. (*Enough for 1 four-pound bird*)

SWEET POTATO STUFFING

4 cups cooked, mashed sweet potatoes
3 tablespoons melted butter
2 eggs, beaten
2 cups toasted fresh bread crumbs
¼ cup chopped green onions
¼ cup chopped celery
1 tablespoon minced fresh parsley
Salt and freshly ground pepper to taste
¼ teaspoon freshly grated nutmeg
¼ teaspoon monosodium glutamate

Combine all the ingredients and mix lightly. (*Enough for 2 four-pound chickens, plus a small casserole*)

SPINACH STUFFING

- 3½ cups cubed day-old white bread
- 4 ten-ounce packages frozen chopped spinach, cooked and drained
- ¼ cup finely chopped celery
- ½ cup finely chopped onion
- 2 tablespoons chopped fresh parsley
- 2 teaspoons poultry seasoning
- 1 teaspoon salt
- Freshly ground pepper to taste

Combine all the ingredients and mix lightly. *(Enough for 1 five-pound bird)*

MUSHROOM-OYSTER STUFFING

- 1 cup chopped canned mushrooms
- 3 large, hard rolls, cubed
- ¼ teaspoon poultry seasoning
- ¼ teaspoon ground mace
- Salt and freshly ground pepper to taste
- ½ cup drained, coarsely chopped oysters
- ¼ cup undiluted cream of mushroom soup
- Sherry, enough to moisten

Combine all the ingredients, blending well. (*Enough for 1 five-pound bird*)

NOODLE-FRUIT STUFFING

- ½ pound egg noodles
- ½ cup chopped onion
- 2 tablespoons butter
- Giblets from a 6-pound chicken, cooked and chopped
- 1 teaspoon salt
- ½ teaspoon ground turmeric
- 1 tablespoon chopped fresh parsley
- 1 large, tart apple, peeled, cored, and chopped
- 1 dozen stewed prunes, drained, pitted, and chopped
- ¼ cup raisins
- 1 tablespoon grated lemon peel
- 1 egg, beaten

Cook the noodles until just tender. Meanwhile, sauté the onion in the butter until it is soft and golden. Drain the noodles, then combine with all the other ingredients in a large bowl and mix lightly. (*Enough for 2 four-pound birds*)

PICKLE-FRUIT STUFFING

- 2½ cups soft bread crumbs
- 1 egg, beaten
- ¼ cup melted butter
- ¼ cup sweet pickle juice
- ¼ cup chopped sweet mixed pickles
- ½ cup chopped dried apricots
- ¼ cup raisins
- ¼ cup chopped walnuts

Combine all the ingredients and mix lightly. (*Enough for 1 four-pound bird*)

SAUERKRAUT-FRUIT STUFFING

⅓ cup chopped onions
2 tablespoons melted butter
1 cup packaged herb stuffing
1 cup drained sauerkraut
½ cup dried apricots, halved and plumped in boiling water
½ cup prunes, pitted and plumped in boiling water
2 tablespoons chopped fresh parsley
1 small bay leaf, crumbled
Salt and freshly ground pepper to taste
¾ teaspoon paprika

Combine all the ingredients and mix lightly. (*Enough for 1 six-pound bird, plus a small casserole*)

CHESTNUT-SAUSAGE STUFFING

1 pound chestnuts
1 pound bulk pork sausage, cooked
Salt and freshly ground pepper to taste
1 onion, minced
1 tablespoon chopped fresh parsley
1 egg, lightly beaten

Using a small, sharp knife, score each chestnut with an X and drop into boiling water for 10 minutes. Peel them while they are hot, using a potholder so you don't burn your fingers, then combine them with all the other ingredients, mixing lightly. (*Enough for 1 six-pound bird*)

OLD-FASHIONED OYSTER STUFFING

7 cups coarse white bread crumbs, packed loosely
Salt and freshly ground pepper to taste
½ teaspoon poultry seasoning
¼ cup (½ stick) butter
Scant ½ cup finely chopped celery
¼ onion, chopped
¾ cup drained, chopped oysters

Combine the bread crumbs and seasonings in a bowl and set aside. Melt the butter in a skillet and sauté the celery and onion until just soft, then stir in the oysters. Pour this mixture over the bread crumb mixture and combine lightly. (*Enough for 1 six-pound bird*)

CRANBERRY STUFFING

1½ cups cranberries
Heaping ¼ cup granulated sugar
¼ cup (½ stick) melted butter
4 cups toasted bread cubes
¾ cup raisins
¾ teaspoon salt
⅛ teaspoon ground cinnamon
2 teaspoons lemon juice
¼ cup chicken stock

Chop the cranberries, then mix lightly with the remaining ingredients. (*Enough for 1 six-pound bird*)

PINEAPPLE GLAZE

- ¼ cup light brown sugar
- ¼ cup catsup
- ½ cup crushed pineapple
- Juice of 1 lemon
- Salt and freshly ground pepper to taste
- 2 tablespoons sherry
- Pinch of freshly grated nutmeg

Combine all the ingredients in a saucepan and heat to the boiling point. Brush the mixture generously over the roasting bird when it is about half done, then brush again several times before removing the bird from the oven. (*Enough to glaze 1 six-pound bird*)

SESAME CRISP GLAZE

- ¼ cup (½ stick) melted butter
- ¼ cup dry white wine
- ½ cup sour cream
- 1 teaspoon paprika
- 1 teaspoon celery salt
- Few grindings of pepper
- 1½ teaspoons Worcestershire sauce
- 1½ tablespoons sesame seeds
- ¾ cup finely chopped pecans

Combine all the ingredients in a saucepan and bring to a boil. Brush the mixture generously over the roasting bird when it is about half done, then brush again several times before removing the bird from the oven. (*Enough to glaze 1 six-pound bird*)

11 Baked Chicken and Casseroles

The Oven: a Many-Splendored Thing

As basic culinary equipment, the oven has no peer. It truly *is* a woman's best friend. When I have prepared a dish for baking, I feel I have the world by the tail. Once having been assembled, most of these recipes can loll about for hours while you get on with other things like chilling the salad plates, polishing the candelabra, or finishing the latest who-dunit.

Even after they have been moved into the oven, these accommodating dishes free your hands for such last-minute *divertissements* as mixing the martinis—and, of course, sampling them.

PART I: VARIATIONS ON BAKED CHICKEN

DHU'S CHICKEN WINO

3 tablespoons butter
All-purpose flour
1 three-pound fryer, disjointed
8 green onions, green tops and all, sliced
1 one-pound can stewed tomatoes
¼ cup chicken broth, more if necessary

½ cup Burgundy, more if necessary
Salt and freshly ground pepper to taste
½ teaspoon Spice Islands Mei Yen seasoning
1 dozen prunes, cooked and pitted

Melt the butter in a flameproof baking dish. Lightly flour the chicken parts and cook in the butter until golden brown. Add the onions and stir until they are limp. Add the tomatoes, chicken broth, wine, and seasonings, then stir and cook for 10 minutes.

Distribute the prunes around the chicken and bake in a 375° oven for 1 hour, or until the chicken is tender, basting several times. If more liquid is required, mix broth and wine in equal parts and spoon over all. (*Serves 4*)

BAKED CHICKEN HILO

2 two-and-one-half-pound fryers, quartered
¼ cup (½ stick) butter
Salt and freshly ground pepper to taste
1¼ cups orange or tangerine juice
½ teaspoon ground cinnamon
½ to 1 teaspoon curry powder, according to taste
⅔ cup blanched slivered almonds
5 tablespoons finely chopped Indian chutney
1 cup canned mandarin orange slices

Place the chicken quarters in a shallow baking pan. Dot them with the butter, sprinkle with salt and pepper, and bake in a 425° oven for about 15 to 20 minutes, or until nicely browned.

In a saucepan, combine the juice, cinnamon, curry powder, almonds, and chutney. Bring to a slow simmer and cook for 10 minutes, then pour over the chicken. Lower the oven heat to 350° and bake for 50 to 60 minutes, or until the chicken is fork tender. Serve on a very hot platter, garnished with the mandarin orange slices. (*Serves 8*)

LADY BIRD'S BIRD

1 cup soy sauce
1 tablespoon minced fresh ginger
1 tablespoon minced green onion
1 tablespoon champagne or wine vinegar
1 three-pound fryer, disjointed
1 large egg, well beaten
2 cups dehydrated potato flakes
Melted butter

Combine the soy sauce, ginger, onion, and vinegar and marinate chicken in the mixture for several hours (the longer the better), turning the pieces several times during the marinating period.

When ready to cook, drain the chicken parts. Dip in the beaten egg, then coat heavily with potato flakes. Place in a shallow baking pan, drizzle some melted butter over, and bake in a 350° oven for about 50 minutes, or until the bird is fork tender. (*Serves 4*)

FEATHERED CLAMBAKE

1 three-pound fryer, disjointed
All-purpose flour
½ cup vegetable oil
1½ cups raw rice
1 cup chopped onion
1 clove garlic, put through a press

- 1 small green pepper, chopped
- 1 one-pound can stewed tomatoes
- 1 eight-ounce bottle clam juice
- 1½ cups water
- Salt and freshly ground pepper to taste
- ⅛ teaspoon dried marjoram
- 2 seven-and-one-half-ounce cans minced clams, undrained
- 1 pound shrimp, cooked, shelled, and deveined
- 1 one-pound can asparagus spears, drained
- Pimiento strips for garnish

Lightly dredge the chicken in the flour, then heat the oil in a large skillet and brown the chicken on both sides. When browned, remove the chicken to a large baking dish. In the same oil, cook the rice, onion, garlic, and green pepper until the rice is golden, then spoon over and around the chicken. In the same frying pan, heat together the tomatoes, clam juice, water, and seasonings. Pour into the baking dish, cover, and bake at 350° for 30 minutes. Add the clams with their liquor, and the shrimp. Cover and bake another 25 minutes. Arrange the asparagus spears over the chicken and decorate with pimiento, then bake for a final 10 minutes. (*Serves 8*)

BAKED CHICKEN, LOW FAT

Not an Oriental dish!

- 1 three-pound fryer, disjointed
- Salt and freshly ground pepper to taste
- 2 teaspoons Hungarian paprika
- 1 tablespoon vegetable oil
- ⅔ cup chicken broth, defatted
- ½ cup chopped white part of leek
- 2 tablespoons minced fresh parsley
- 1 eight-ounce container imitation sour cream

Sprinkle the chicken parts with salt, pepper, and paprika. Lightly grease a shallow baking pan with the oil. Place the chicken parts in the pan, skin side up, and bake for 15 minutes in a 400° oven. Add the broth, leeks, and parsley, then cover the pan loosely with foil and reduce the heat to 325° for about 45 minutes, or until all the chicken parts are tender.

When tender, remove the foil and turn the heat up to 350° to brown the chicken, which should take only a few minutes, then remove the chicken to a heated platter and keep hot. Pour all the juices into a saucepan, stirring and scraping up all the nice crunchy bits. Heat gently as you stir in the imitation sour cream. Pour the sauce over and serve. (*Serves 4 to 6*)

CHICKEN CAPRI

1 eight-ounce package herbed croutons, rolled into crumbs
Salt and freshly ground pepper to taste
½ cup freshly grated, mixed Parmesan and Romano cheese
½ teaspoon garlic powder
1 three-pound fryer, disjointed
¾ cup evaporated milk
Melted butter

Pour the crouton crumbs into a paper bag, along with salt, pepper, grated cheese, and garlic powder. Dip the chicken parts into the milk, shake off excess liquid, then shake in the bag until coated with crumbs. Put the chicken into a shallow baking pan, drizzle with melted butter, and bake in a 350° oven for about 50 minutes, or until tender. (*Serves 4*)

STICKY CHICKEN

- 1 three-pound fryer, disjointed
- All-purpose flour
- ¼ cup vegetable oil
- 1 package onion soup mix
- 1 one-pound can stewed tomatoes
- 1 cup dry white wine
- Freshly ground pepper to taste (optional)
- ½ pound mozzarella cheese, shredded

Dredge the chicken in flour and brown on both sides in the oil in a heavy skillet, then transfer to a shallow baking pan. Blend the soup mix, tomatoes, wine, and pepper, if desired, and pour over the chicken. Bake at 325° for about 1 hour.

Fifteen minutes before the chicken is fork tender, sprinkle the cheese over it. (*Serves 4 to 6*)

Note: Use paper napkins *only* with this dish.

BAKED CHICKEN TARRAGON

- 5 tablespoons butter
- 1 three-pound fryer, left whole
- Salt and freshly ground pepper to taste
- 1 teaspoon dried tarragon, crushed
- 1 carrot, chopped
- 4 green onions, chopped
- ½ cup chicken broth
- ½ cup dry white wine

Heat 4 tablespoons of the butter in a Dutch oven and brown the chicken on all sides. Combine the salt, pepper, tarragon, carrot, and onion, and then cut in the remaining tablespoon of butter. Taste for seasoning, then lightly stuff the cavity of the chicken with the dressing. Blend the broth and wine and pour it around chicken, then cover and roast in a 350° oven for about 50 minutes, or until the bird is fork tender. Quarter the chicken and serve each portion with dressing and with pan juices poured over. (*Serves 4*)

OVEN-BARBECUED CHICKEN I

¾ cup (1½ sticks) butter
2 cups yellow cornmeal
1 tablespoon salt
5 teaspoons powdered barbecue seasoning
1 two-and-one-half- to three-pound fryer, disjointed
1 egg, lightly beaten
¾ cup tomato juice

Preheat the oven to 400°, then melt the butter in a large, shallow pan in the oven. Combine the cornmeal, salt, and barbecue seasoning in a paper bag. Shake the chicken, a couple of pieces at a time, in the bag to coat it evenly. Dip in a mixture of egg and tomato juice, then shake again in the cornmeal mix.

Place the coated chicken pieces, skin side down, in a single layer in the melted butter.

Bake for 30 minutes, then turn the pieces and bake another half hour, until the chicken is tender and golden brown. (*Serves 4*)

Note: If it's a warm summer day, you might chill the dish and serve the chicken cold for a change.

OVEN-BARBECUED CHICKEN II

1 three-pound fryer, quartered
All-purpose flour
Salt and freshly ground pepper to taste
4 thick slices bacon
1 four-and-one-half-ounce can sliced mushrooms, undrained
Bottled barbecue sauce

Shake the chicken pieces in a paper bag with the flour, salt, and pepper. Place in a shallow baking pan, then top each piece with a bacon slice. Cover the pan with foil and bake in a 400° oven for 40 minutes, then uncover and pour the undrained mushrooms over chicken. Streak with barbecue sauce, cover once more, and bake another 10 minutes. Uncover and place under the broiler until the chicken is lightly browned. (*Serves 4*)

OVEN-BARBECUED CHICKEN III

1 six-ounce can frozen lemonade concentrate
¾ cup bottled barbecue sauce
1 three-pound fryer, disjointed

Defrost the lemonade concentrate and mix with the barbecue sauce. Slather the chicken parts with the mixture and bake in a shallow pan in a 350° oven for 45 minutes, or until the chicken is tender, basting frequently. (*Serves 4*)

BALINESE CHICKEN

1 three-pound fryer, disjointed
All-purpose flour
¼ cup peanut oil

- 2 large, sweet onions, cut up
- 2 medium oranges, washed, cut up, and seeded
- ½ cup raw rice
- 1 cup chopped pecans
- 1½ cups half-and-half
- 1 teaspoon salt
- Freshly ground pepper to taste
- ⅓ teaspoon dried thyme
- Pinch of cayenne
- ¼ teaspoon granulated sugar

Dust the chicken parts with flour and brown lightly in the hot oil, then remove to a warm platter and set aside. Put the onions and oranges, including the peel, through a food grinder and set aside. Add the rice and pecans to the drippings in the pan in which the chicken was browned and cook gently, stirring, until the rice is dark gold. Add the onion-orange mixture and blend well.

Spread the mixture evenly on the bottom of a medium-deep baking pan, arrange the chicken parts on top, and pour half-and-half over all. Mix together the salt, pepper, thyme, cayenne, and sugar and sprinkle evenly over the top. Cover tightly and bake in a 350° oven for 1 hour. (*Serves 4 to 6*)

CHICKEN PIERRE

- 1 three-pound fryer, quartered
- All-purpose flour
- ¼ cup peanut oil
- 4 shallots, chopped
- 6 large mushrooms, stems and all, sliced
- ¾ cup dry white wine
- Salt and freshly ground pepper to taste
- ½ cup chicken broth
- 2 small bay leaves
- ¼ teaspoon poultry seasoning

Dust the chicken with flour and brown on both sides in hot peanut oil, then remove to a baking dish. In the same oil, sauté the shallots and mushrooms until golden. Add the wine, salt, pepper, and chicken broth and cook another 5 minutes. Strain the sauce, then pour it over the chicken, lay bay leaves on top and sprinkle with poultry seasoning. Bake in a 350° oven about 30 minutes, or until chicken is tender. (*Serves 4*)

SNAP-E-TOM BAKE

1 three-pound fryer, disjointed
½ cup all-purpose flour
¼ cup butter
1 eight-ounce can Snap-E-Tom (or V-8 juice spiced with 2 or 3 drops of Tabasco)
¼ cup India relish
1½ teaspoons Worcestershire sauce
2 small bay leaves

Lightly dredge the chicken parts in the flour. Melt the butter in a skillet and quickly brown the chicken, then remove to a flattish baking dish. Combine the remaining ingredients in the same skillet and cook, stirring constantly, until well blended and very hot. Pour over the chicken, then bake in a 350° oven for about 30 minutes, or until the chicken is tender. (*Serves 4*)

TAMAR'S BAKED CHICKEN

1 three-pound fryer, disjointed
1 large green pepper, chopped

2 medium onions, chopped
2 cloves garlic, put through a press
2 fresh tomatoes, chopped
Salt and freshly ground pepper to taste
2 teaspoons curry powder
2 teaspoons ground coriander
¼ teaspoon ground cinnamon
¼ teaspoon ground turmeric
¼ cup (½ stick) melted butter
1 cup chicken broth

Place the chicken in a shallow baking pan. Combine the green pepper, onion, garlic, and tomato and spread over the chicken, then sprinkle with the combined salt, pepper, and spices. Drizzle the melted butter over all, then cover and allow the flavors to blend for 2 to 3 hours.

When ready to cook, pour the chicken broth around the chicken and bake in a 375° oven for 1 hour. (*Serves 4 to 6*)

BAKED CHICKEN FRICASSEE

¾ cup all-purpose flour
2 tablespoons cornstarch
2 teaspoons paprika
¼ teaspoon dried marjoram
1 teaspoon salt
Freshly ground pepper to taste
1 three-pound fryer, disjointed
6 green onions, minced
3 teaspoons minced fresh parsley
1 clove garlic, put through a press
1 ten-and-one-half-ounce can cream of mushroom soup
1 soup can milk or half-and-half

Combine the flour, cornstarch, paprika, marjoram, salt, and pepper in a paper bag, then shake the chicken parts in the mixture. Shake off the excess flour and lay the chicken pieces in a baking pan of medium depth, then cover with the onions, parsley, and garlic. Combine the mushroom soup and milk and pour over the chicken.

Bake the chicken, uncovered, in a 375° oven for 30 minutes, or until nicely browned. Cover and reduce the heat to 350° for 30 minutes, or until the chicken is tender. To crisp the fowl, uncover and raise the heat to 400° for about 10 minutes. (*Serves 4 to 6*)

CHICKEN BAKED WITH PEANUTS

1 teaspoon salt
Freshly ground pepper to taste
½ teaspoon poultry seasoning
1 whole egg, beaten
½ cup smooth or crunchy peanut butter
6 tablespoons milk or half-and-half, more if necessary
1 three-and-one-half-pound fryer, disjointed
6 tablespoons cornstarch
⅔ cup fresh bread crumbs
½ cup (1 stick) melted butter

Combine the seasonings, egg, and peanut butter in a bowl. Add the milk gradually and beat until the mixture is very smooth. (If it appears too thick, add a little more milk.) Dust the chicken parts with the cornstarch and dip into peanut butter mixture, then into the bread crumbs. Place in a shallow baking pan and drizzle with the melted butter. Bake, uncovered, in a 350° oven for 50 minutes, or until the chicken is tender. (*Serves 4 to 6*)

GLAMOUR CHICKEN

1 three-pound chicken, disjointed
½ cup (1 stick) melted butter
1½ tablespoons Escoffier's Sauce Diable
1 cup sour cream
1 three-ounce package cream cheese
½ cup dry white wine
Salt and freshly ground pepper to taste
½ teaspoon paprika

Place the chicken parts in a baking pan and brush generously with a mixture of the melted butter and Sauce Diable. Combine the sour cream, cream cheese, wine, and seasonings in a blender container and whir until smooth. Pour over the chicken parts and bake in a 325° oven for 1½ hours, or until the chicken is fork tender. Use pan juices as a sauce. (*Serves 4 to 6*)

BAKED CHICKEN PINEAPPLE

Salt and freshly ground pepper to taste
1 teaspoon dried rosemary, crushed
1 three-pound fryer, disjointed
12 green onions, thinly sliced
1 cup pineapple juice
1½ teaspoons minced candied ginger
4 slices pineapple, halved

Combine the salt, pepper, and rosemary and rub the chicken parts thoroughly with the mixture, lifting the skin and rubbing the seasoning into the flesh. Place the chicken in a shallow baking pan and sprinkle with the sliced onions, then mix the juice and candied ginger and pour over all. Bake, uncovered, in a 375° oven for about 50 minutes, basting frequently. Fifteen minutes before the chicken is done, arrange the pineapple slices on top. Finish baking, uncovered. (*Serves 4 to 6*)

PART II: A CLUTCH OF CASSEROLES—OR DINNERS-IN-A-DISH

CHICKEN AND RICE CUSTARD

6 eggs
3 cups half-and-half
Salt and freshly ground pepper to taste
⅔ teaspoon poultry seasoning
2½ to 3 cups cooked rice
2½ to 3 cups diced, cooked chicken
⅓ cup chopped green onions

Beat eggs to a froth, then beat in the milk, along with the salt, pepper, and poultry seasoning. Stir in the rice, chicken, and minced onion. Spoon into a casserole and set the dish in a pan of hot water. Bake at 325° for about 1 hour, or until a knife inserted in the center comes out clean. (*Serves 6 to 8*)

CHICKEN UNDER CROUTONS

- 4 cups cooked noodles
- 1½ cups grated sharp cheese
- 5 tablespoons butter
- 1 onion, minced
- 1 four-ounce jar pimientos, drained and diced
- 4 cups diced, cooked chicken
- ½ pound smoked tongue, slivered
- 2 cups chicken broth
- 1 clove garlic, put through a press
- 1½ cups toasted croutons

While the noodles are still hot, combine with the cheese, 2 tablespoons of the butter, the onion, and pimientos. Combine the chicken and tongue. Layer a large casserole with the noodle mixture and the chicken-tongue mixture, ending with noodles. Pour in the chicken broth. Melt the remaining 3 tablespoons butter in a saucepan with the garlic and pour over the toasted croutons. Sprinkle the croutons on top of the casserole and bake in a 350° oven for about 40 minutes, or until bubbling. *(Serves 8)*

DIVINE CHICKEN DIVAN

- 1 five-pound roasting hen, left whole
- Salt to taste
- 1 ten-and-one-half-ounce can cream of celery soup, undiluted
- ¼ cup milk
- ¼ teaspoon nutmeg
- ½ cup mayonnaise
- 3 tablespoons sherry
- 1 teaspoon Worcestershire sauce

½ cup heavy cream, whipped
2 ten-ounce packages frozen broccoli or equivalent amount of fresh broccoli, cooked
1 cup grated Parmesan cheese

Cook the chicken in water to cover, salted to taste, until tender (about 1½ hours). Allow to cool quickly. Meanwhile, heat the soup, milk, and nutmeg in a saucepan, then combine with the mayonnaise, sherry and Worcestershire, then fold in the whipped cream.

Arrange the cooked broccoli in the bottom of a large casserole and sprinkle with half the Parmesan. Skin and slice the chicken and lay the meat over the broccoli. Cover with sauce, top with the remaining cheese, and bake in a 350° oven until hot and bubbling. Brown under the broiler and serve immediately. (*Serves 6 to 8*)

SPAGHETTI-CHICKEN CASSEROLE

3 cups cooked, rinsed, and drained spaghetti
1 onion, chopped
2 cloves garlic, put through a press
2 tablespoons butter
2½ cups canned stewed tomatoes
Salt and freshly ground pepper to taste
1 tablespoon granulated sugar
Pinch of cayenne
1¼ cups sliced, sautéed mushrooms
2½ cups diced, cooked chicken
1 cup freshly grated, mixed Parmesan and Romano cheese

Place the spaghetti in a buttered casserole and set aside. Sauté the onion and garlic in the butter until limp, then add the stewed tomatoes, salt, pepper, sugar, and cayenne. Heat to the boiling point, then lower the heat and add the mushrooms and chicken. Pour over the spaghetti in the casserole and toss with two forks until well mixed. Sprinkle the top with the grated cheese and bake in a 350° oven until heated through and the cheese is lightly browned. (*Serves 6*)

LIGHT-HEADED CHICKEN

A good luncheon dish.

1 ten-and-one-half-ounce can condensed cream of mushroom soup, undiluted
⅓ cup milk
½ teaspoon salt
1 cup diced, cooked chicken
2 cups cooked French-cut green beans
4 eggs, separated
⅓ cup grated Cheddar cheese

Combine the soup, milk, and salt in a smallish casserole. Add the chicken and beans and bake for 10 minutes in a 375° oven.

Meanwhile, beat the egg whites until stiff peaks form. Beat the egg yolks in a separate bowl and add the cheese, then lightly fold the cheese-yolk mixture into the whites and mound on the chicken mixture. Bake an additional 30 minutes, or until lightly browned. (*Serves 4*)

CREOLE CASSEROLE

1 three-pound fryer, disjointed
Salt and freshly ground pepper to taste
¼ cup (½ stick) butter
1 onion, chopped

- 3 cups cooked rice
- 1 ten-ounce package frozen peas, thawed
- 2 cups canned stewed tomatoes
- ¼ cup freshly grated, mixed Parmesan and Romano cheese

Sprinkle the chicken parts with salt and pepper, then brown on both sides in the butter. Add the onion and continue cooking until the onion is limp. Place the rice in a 3-quart casserole and add the peas in an even layer, then top with the chicken parts and onion and pour the tomatoes over all. Top with the cheese. Cover and bake in a 350° oven for about 1 hour, or until the chicken is fork tender. (*Serves 4 to 6*)

CASSEROLE TÍA JUANA

- 1 three-pound fryer, disjointed
- Salt and freshly ground pepper to taste
- ¼ cup peanut oil
- 1 medium-sized onion, chopped
- 2 cups raw rice
- 4 cups chicken broth
- 2 tomatoes, chopped
- 2 small carrots, chopped
- ½ cup sliced ripe olives
- 1 cup pitted prunes
- ½ cup seedless raisins
- ¼ teaspoon dried oregano
- 1 ten-ounce package frozen peas, cooked

Season the chicken with salt and pepper and brown lightly on both sides in the hot oil. Transfer to a 3-quart casserole. Add the onion to the same oil and cook until limp. Add the rice and cook, stirring constantly, until golden, then add the chicken broth, tomatoes, carrots, olives, prunes, and raisins.

Stir in the oregano and bring to a boil, stirring to blend all the ingredients. Pour over the chicken.

Cover the casserole and bake in a 350° oven until the chicken is tender (about 50 minutes). Stir the cooked peas into the rice mixture and continue cooking until the rice is fluffy and dry. (*Serves 6*)

COMPANY CASSEROLE

2 tablespoons butter
2 tablespoons all-purpose flour
¼ teaspoon prepared mustard
1 teaspoon salt
Freshly ground pepper to taste
2 cups milk
1 cup grated Cheddar cheese
1 ten-ounce package frozen broccoli, cooked
¼ pound noodles, cooked
2 cups diced, cooked chicken
⅓ cup toasted, slivered almonds

In a saucepan over low heat, melt the butter. Blend in the flour, mustard, salt, and pepper. Add the milk and cook, stirring constantly, until thickened. Remove from the heat and stir in the cheese until it melts.

Dice the broccoli stems, then arrange the noodles, broccoli stems, and chicken in a shallow casserole. Pour the cheese sauce over all. Arrange the broccoli flowers on top, pressing lightly into the sauce. Sprinkle with the almonds and bake in a 350° oven until bubbly. (*Serves 4 to 6*)

CHICKEN-ARTICHOKE CASSEROLE

¼ cup (½ stick) butter
¼ cup all-purpose flour
1 cup half-and-half
1 cup chicken broth
⅔ cup grated Tillamook cheese
¼ cup sherry
Salt and freshly ground pepper to taste
3 cups diced, cooked chicken
2 ten-ounce packages frozen artichoke hearts, cooked

In a saucepan over low heat, melt the butter, then blend in the flour until smooth. Gradually add the half-and-half and chicken broth, stirring constantly until smooth and thick. Remove from the heat and stir in half the cheese and all the sherry. Add salt and pepper.

Layer the chicken and cooked artichoke hearts in a 3-quart casserole, then pour the cheese sauce over all and sprinkle the remaining cheese on top. Bake in a 375° oven for about 20 minutes, or until cheese melts and bubbles. (*Serves 6 to 8*)

CHICKEN-HAM JAMBALAYA

2 tablespoons bacon fat
1 cup chopped onion
1 cup chopped green pepper
2 cloves garlic, put through a press
¾ pound pork sausage links, cut in fourths
1½ cups diced, cooked chicken
1¼ cups diced, cooked ham
2½ cups cut-up canned tomatoes

1 cup raw rice
2 cups chicken broth
1½ tablespoons minced fresh parsley
½ teaspoon chili powder
Salt and freshly ground pepper to taste

Melt the bacon fat in a large skillet and sauté the onion, green pepper, and garlic, stirring frequently so the garlic does not brown. When the vegetables are fairly tender, add the sausage quarters and cook for 5 minutes, turning them so they cook evenly. Add the chicken and ham and cook for 5 minutes, then add the remaining ingredients and mix together well.

Transfer to a 3- or 4-quart casserole, cover, and bake in a 350° oven for 50 to 60 minutes, or until the rice has absorbed all the liquid and is fluffy and dry. (*Serves 8*)

NOVAK'S NAMELESS WONDER

Chicken Filling

2 cups diced, cooked chicken
2 cups diced, cooked ham
4 hard-cooked eggs, sliced
2 cups cooked small white onions
1 ten-and-one-half-ounce can cream of mushroom soup, undiluted
½ cup half-and-half
1 teaspoon curry powder
1½ tablespoons chopped fresh parsley

Sweet Potato Crust

1⅓ cups all-purpose flour
1½ teaspoons salt
3 teaspoons baking powder

¼ cup (½ stick) butter
1 cup cooked, mashed sweet potatoes
¼ cup milk

Combine all the ingredients for the filling and place in a 3-quart casserole. Set aside while you prepare the sweet potato crust.

Sift together 1 cup of the flour, the salt, and baking powder. With 2 knives or a pastry blender, cut in the shortening until the mixture resembles small peas. Blend in the sweet potato, then mix in the milk with a fork. Spread the remaining flour on a board, then press the dough out on the board to a thickness of ½ inch. Cut in star shapes with a cookie cutter, then place the shapes on top of the casserole and bake in a 450° oven for 20 minutes. (*Serves 8*)

ORIENTAL CHICKEN CASSEROLE

1 cup diagonally sliced celery
½ cup diagonally sliced green onions
⅓ cup butter
¼ cup all-purpose flour
1 teaspoon salt
Pinch of garlic salt
2 cups milk
2 teaspoons soy sauce
½ cup shredded Cheddar cheese
2 cups diced, cooked chicken
1 8-ounce can water chestnuts, sliced
1 6-ounce can chow mein noodles

Sauté the celery and onions in the butter until the onions are soft, then blend in the flour and salts. Add the milk and soy sauce, stirring constantly, and cook until thickened. Remove from the heat and add the cheese, stirring until melted, then stir in the chicken and water chestnuts.

Arrange alternate layers of noodles and chicken mixture in a 1½-quart casserole, beginning and ending with noodles. Bake in a 375° oven for 25 to 30 minutes, or until hot and bubbly. (*Serves 6*)

PAPA'S CHICKEN PAPRIKASH

1 three-and-one-half-pound fryer, disjointed
¼ cup butter
½ cup chopped onion
¼ cup all-purpose flour
2 tablespoons Hungarian paprika
2 teaspoons salt
¼ teaspoon freshly ground pepper
1¾ cups chicken broth
2 cups sour cream
1 tablespoon Worcestershire sauce
½ pound noodles, cooked

Brown the chicken in the butter in a large skillet, then remove and set aside. Add the onion to the pan drippings and blend in the flour, paprika, salt, and pepper. Add the broth and cook, stirring, until thick and smooth, then stir in the sour cream and Worcestershire sauce.

Mix half the sauce with the cooked noodles and pour into a shallow 3-quart casserole. Arrange the chicken on top, spoon the remaining sauce over the chicken, and bake at 325° for 1 hour, or until the chicken is tender. (*Serves 6*)

CORNY CHICKEN CASSEROLE

- 1 fifteen-ounce can tomato sauce
- 1 tablespoon lemon juice
- 1 egg, beaten
- 2 cups diced, cooked chicken
- 1 cup crushed corn chips
- ½ cup chopped celery
- 1 teaspoon minced onion
- 1 tablespoon chopped green pepper
- 1 eight-ounce can whole-kernel corn, drained
- 1 teaspoon Worcestershire sauce
- ½ teaspoon salt

Blend the tomato sauce, lemon juice, and egg, then add the remaining ingredients and mix lightly but thoroughly. Turn into a 1½-quart casserole, cover, and bake at 325° for about 1 hour. (*Serves 6*)

PRONTO CASSEROLE

- 1 ten-and-one-half-ounce can cream of mushroom soup
- ⅓ cup white wine
- 1 cup diced, cooked chicken
- 2 hard-cooked eggs, sliced
- Spice Islands Beau Monde Seasoning to taste
- Crushed potato chips

Blend the soup and wine, then add all the other ingredients except the crushed potato chips. Taste for seasoning, then place in a 1½-quart casserole and top with the potato chips. Bake at 375° for about 30 minutes. (*Serves 4*)

DOWN EAST CASSEROLE

- 2 two-pound fryers, split down the back
- Flour
- Salt and freshly ground pepper
- ¼ cup (½ stick) butter
- 1½ cups boiling water
- 1 cup cream or evaporated milk
- 2 cups drained oysters

Dredge the chickens in flour seasoned with salt and pepper, then lay them, skin side up, in a deep casserole. Dot with the butter. Pour the boiling water into the casserole, cover, and bake at 350° for 50 minutes, or until the chicken is tender. Pour the cream over birds, then add the drained oysters. Cover and cook briefly, just until oysters are curled at the edges. (*Serves 4*)

Note: Can you manage homemade bread? It's almost a must with this dish!

CHICKEN-SAUSAGE CASSEROLE

- 16 pieces of chicken (assorted breasts, thighs, and drumsticks)
- ½ cup all-purpose flour
- 2 teaspoons salt
- ¼ teaspoon freshly ground pepper
- 3 tablespoons butter
- 3 tablespoons corn oil
- 1 quart chicken broth
- Pinch of dried tarragon
- 1 bay leaf, crushed
- 2 cloves garlic, put through a press
- 16 small white onions, peeled
- 2 seven-ounce cans miniature cocktail sausages
- ½ pound mushrooms, sliced

Dust the chicken parts with a mixture of ¼ cup flour, salt, and pepper. Brown well in the butter and oil, then transfer the chicken to a 3- to 4-quart casserole. To the juices in browning pan, add the remaining ¼ cup flour and blend thoroughly. Gradually add the chicken broth, stirring with a whisk until smooth, then add the tarragon, bay leaf, and garlic.

To the chicken in the casserole, add the onions and sausages. Be sure the gravy in the pan is velvety smooth, then pour it over the chicken. Cover and bake at 350° for 1 hour, then add the mushrooms and bake another 20 minutes, or until the chicken and vegetables are tender. (*Serves 8*)

CHICKEN CASSEROLE ALSACE

1 one-and-one-half-pound slice of ham, with some fat, cubed
1 clove garlic, put through a press
6 green onions, chopped fine
2 two-and-one-half-pound chickens, trussed for baking
1 large white cabbage, quartered
2 cups rich chicken stock
½ cup dry white wine
1 tablespoon brandy

Brown the ham cubes in a large skillet with the garlic and onions. When enough fat has been rendered, brown the chickens in the pan.

Place the cabbage in a deep casserole and pour the chicken stock over it, then place the chickens, ham, and onions on top. Cover and bake in a 350° oven for about 1½ hours, or until the chicken is tender. Just before serving, stir in the wine and brandy. (*Serves 8*)

CHICKEN OLÉ

1 fifteen-ounce can chicken tamales
1 cup diced, cooked chicken
1 eight-ounce can creamed corn
½ cup chopped sweet pickles
Salt and freshly ground pepper to taste
Worcestershire sauce to taste
¼ cup (½ stick) butter
½ pound Monterey Jack cheese, grated

Combine all the ingredients except the butter and cheese and place in an earthenware casserole. Dot liberally with the butter and top with the grated cheese, then bake in a 400° oven for about 20 to 25 minutes. (*Serves 4 to 6*)

QUICK CASSOULET

3 chicken breasts, boned and skinned
1 pound pork sausage links, halved
1 pound pork loin, cut in large cubes
3 knockwurst, cut into 1-inch pieces
1½ pounds boneless leg of lamb, cut in large cubes
1 cup minced onion
3 cloves garlic, put through a press
3 twenty-ounce cans baked beans, drained
1 twenty-ounce can kidney beans, drained
¼ teaspoon dried oregano, crushed
2 cups dry white wine

Cut the chicken breasts in half lengthwise, then into narrow strips, and set aside. Brown the pork sausage in a large skillet, then add the pork, knockwurst, lamb, and chicken, stirring all together. Add the onion and garlic and cook until onion is lightly browned, then add the beans and stir in the oregano and wine. When the mixture is well blended, transfer to a large earthenware casserole and bake in a 350° oven for 1½ hours. Sourdough French rolls and a crisp green salad are splendid accompaniments. (*Serves 8 to 10*)

CHICKEN-ENDIVE CASSEROLE

8 fresh Belgian endive
¼ cup (½ stick) butter
1 cup beef bouillon
1 four-pound roasting chicken, quartered
1 good-sized ham steak, quartered
½ pound Cheddar cheese, grated
Salt and freshly ground pepper to taste

Braise the endive in 2 tablespoons of the butter and the bouillon for 5 minutes, then set aside. Heat the remaining butter in a heavy skillet and brown the chicken parts on all sides, then arrange in a well-greased casserole. Place a piece of ham on each chicken quarter and tuck the endive in between. Pour the liquid from the endive over all and top with the shredded cheese. Sprinkle with salt and pepper, cover, and bake in a 375° oven for 40 minutes or more, or until the chicken is tender. Remove the casserole cover for the last 15 minutes of cooking to allow the chicken to get crispy. (*Serves 4*)

12 Broiled Chicken and Marinades

Speaking of broiled chicken, my personal preference for crunchy skin and moist meat is the dieter's despair. I firmly believe in *lots* of butter and/or margarine. The dried-out broiler is definitely not for me!

The procedure is virtually the same for all the following recipes (any deviation will be so noted in the individual instructions). *Always follow these three rules:* (1) Skin side down first; (2) moderate heat; (3) liberal basting every 5 minutes!

BASIC BROILED CHICKEN, CHEZ MOI

2 two-and-one-half-pound broilers, quartered
½ cup (1 stick) melted butter
Lemon juice, herb seasoning, A-1 Sauce, or dried rosemary leaves

Rub the chicken quarters with a mixture of butter and any of the suggested seasonings. Place in a broiling pan, skin side down, and adjust so that the chicken is no less than 5, no more than 6, inches from the source of heat. Broil under moderate heat, swabbing the chicken generously with the butter mixture every 5 minutes for 15 minutes, then turn skin side up and broil, swabbing again every 5 minutes, for 15 to 20 minutes, or until the chicken is tender. (*Serves 8*)

BARBECUE-BROILED CHICKEN

3 broilers, halved
1 sixteen-ounce bottle barbecue sauce of your choice

Arrange the chicken halves on a broiler pan, skin side down, and swab liberally with sauce. Place the pan under the broiler so that the chicken is 5 inches from the heat source and broil under moderate heat for 15 minutes, basting every 5 minutes. Turn the chicken skin side up and repeat the broiling procedure until the chicken is tender (15 to 20 minutes). (*Serves 6*)

CHEESE-BROILED CHICKEN

3 tablespoons butter
3 tablespoons lemon juice
Salt and freshly ground pepper to taste
¼ teaspoon poultry seasoning
3 broilers, halved
¾ cup grated Swiss cheese

Melt the butter in a small saucepan and add the lemon juice, salt, pepper, and poultry seasoning. Swab the chicken liberally with the sauce, then follow the basic broiling directions (page 135), cutting down 5 minutes on the final timing so the birds can be sprinkled with the grated cheese. Return to the broiler just until the cheese melts and bubbles. (*Serves 6*)

FLAMED BROILERS

3 broilers, halved
¼ cup peanut oil
1 clove garlic, put through a press
Salt and freshly ground pepper to taste
1 teaspoon A-1 Sauce
1 cup vodka, slightly warmed

Swab the chicken halves with a mixture of the oil, garlic, salt, pepper, and A-1 Sauce. Proceed as directed on page 135 for broiling. When the chicken is tender, place in a single layer in a very hot, flameproof dish. Pour the vodka over all and set aflame. (Since where flambéed dishes are concerned I am definitely chicken, I keep away from the inevitable "explosion" by using a very long fireplace match, and strongly recommend you do the same!) Bring to the table while the flames are still dramatically bright, and serve at once. (*Serves 6*)

APRICOT-CHICKEN BROIL

2 broilers, halved
1 one-pound can large apricot halves, drained but ½ cup juice reserved
½ cup white wine
1 cup catsup
¼ cup vegetable oil
3 drops Tabasco

Marinate the chicken in a combination of all the ingredients except the apricot halves. For best results allow *at least 2 hours*, preferably longer. Broil as recommended on page 135, then, during the final swabbing, place the apricot halves alongside the chicken on the broiler pan and cook until the chicken is tender. Serve, garnished with the apricots. (*Serves 4*)

CHICKEN PANCHO

- 2 broilers, halved
- 1 eight-ounce can tomato sauce
- ¼ cup vegetable oil
- 1 tablespoon finely chopped canned, peeled green chili
- ¼ cup wine vinegar
- 1 small whole clove garlic, put through a press
- 1 teaspoon liquid smoke
- 1 teaspoon onion powder
- ½ cup grated sharp Cheddar cheese

Put the chicken in a deep bowl, then combine all the other ingredients except the cheese and pour over. Allow the chicken to marinate, covered, overnight in the refrigerator. Broil as recommended on page 135, but about 5 minutes before the chicken has finished cooking, spread the halves with grated cheese. Allow the cheese to melt and bubble and serve at once. (*Serves 4*)

PARMESAN BROILERS

- 3 broilers, halved
- Salt and freshly ground pepper to taste
- Garlic salt to taste
- 1 cup (2 sticks) melted butter
- ½ cup freshly grated Parmesan cheese
- 1 clove garlic, put through a press

Broil the chicken as recommended on page 135, basting frequently with a blend of the remaining ingredients. (*Serves 6*)

CHICKEN WITH PARMESAN PEARS

- **3 broilers, halved**
- **Vegetable oil**
- **Seasoned salt**
- **2 strips bacon**
- **½ green pepper, chopped fine**
- **¼ cup buttered bread crumbs**
- **¼ cup freshly grated Parmesan cheese**
- **3 ripe, firm pears, pared and cored**

Broil the chicken as recommended on page 135, swabbing liberally with the oil mixed with the seasoned salt.

While the chicken cooks, fry the bacon in a skillet until it is crisp, then remove. Cook the green pepper in the pan drippings until just tender, then mix with crumbled bacon, bread crumbs, and cheese. When you turn the chicken skin side up, place the pear halves on broiler rack and cover them completely with the bacon-cheese mixture. Continue broiling the chicken until it is done. (*Serves 6*)

SAFFRON BROIL

- **2 broilers, halved**
- **¼ cup olive oil**
- **1 tablespoon lemon juice**
- **½ teaspoon salt**
- **¼ teaspoon saffron**

Marinate the chicken halves in a mixture of the remaining ingredients for an hour or two before broiling as directed on page 135. Baste copiously with the marinade during the cooking process. (*Serves 4*)

MARINATED BROILERS

- 2 broilers, halved
- 1 eight-ounce bottle Italian salad dressing with cheese
- Salt and freshly ground pepper to taste
- 8 thick slices fresh tomato
- Butter
- ¼ teaspoon dried sweet basil

Marinate the chicken in the salad dressing for at least 2 hours, then season with salt and pepper and broil as recommended on page 135. About 7 minutes before the chicken is done, surround with the tomato slices. Dot each slice with butter and sprinkle with sweet basil. Serve the chicken garnished with the broiled tomato slices. (*Serves 4*)

SOUTH SEA BROILERS

- 2 broilers, halved
- Salt and freshly ground pepper to taste
- ⅓ cup melted butter
- 2 teaspoons Worcestershire sauce
- ½ cup orange juice
- ½ cup pineapple juice
- 3 teaspoons lemon juice
- 1 tablespoon arrowroot
- ⅔ cup ground macadamia nuts

Season the chicken with salt and pepper, then brush with a mixture of the melted butter and Worcestershire sauce. Broil as recommended on page 135.

Meanwhile, blend all the juices in a small saucepan and heat over a low flame. Blend in the arrowroot until the sauce thickens. When the chicken has finished cooking, serve it drenched in the fruit sauce and sprinkled with the ground nuts. (*Serves 4*)

CHICKEN KEBABS

- **6 chicken breasts, boned, skinned, and cut into 1-inch squares**
- **5 cloves garlic, put through a press**
- **2 tablespoons minced fresh parsley**
- **½ cup vegetable oil**
- **1½ tablespoons wine vinegar**
- **1 tablespoon soy sauce**
- **2 teaspoons monosodium glutamate**
- **¼ cup sherry**
- **Salt and freshly ground pepper to taste**
- **8 strips of bacon, cut into thirds**
- **24 cherry tomatoes**

Place the squares of chicken in a bowl and add all the other ingredients except the bacon and tomatoes. Mix well and allow to marinate for at least 2 hours.

When ready to cook, drain the chicken squares, reserving the marinade, then wrap each square in a piece of bacon and thread on 6 metal or bamboo skewers, placing a cherry tomato between every 2 pieces of bacon-wrapped chicken. Brush the remaining marinade over the skewers and place under a preheated broiler. Broil 2 inches from the heat source for about 4 minutes, or until the bacon is cooked. Turn and repeat the process, then serve immediately. (*Serves 6*)

JAPANESE KEBABS

- **1 three- to four-pound broiler, boned and cut into 1½-inch squares**
- **Cayenne to taste**
- **¾ cup shoyu (Japanese soy sauce)**
- **¼ cup granulated sugar**
- **¾ cup sake (rice wine)**
- **10 scallions, green part and all, cut into 2-inch lengths**

Marinate the chicken in a mixture of the cayenne, shoyu, sugar, and sake for about 1 hour. When ready to cook, drain the chicken squares and reserve the marinade. Thread the chicken and scallions on metal or bamboo skewers, allowing 4 pieces of chicken to every 3 of scallions. Baste well with the sauce and broil 2 inches from the heat source, about 4 minutes on each side. *(Serves 4 to 6)*

THREE BROILER BASTES

These are equally good for chicken on the grill.

I

¼ cup (½ stick) butter
Salt and freshly ground pepper to taste
1 teaspoon dried chervil
1 cup dry white wine
Paprika

II

½ cup vegetable oil
2 tablespoons lemon juice
¼ teaspoon freshly ground pepper
¼ teaspoon onion salt
¼ teaspoon poultry seasoning
2 teaspoons salt

III

¼ cup (½ stick) butter
1 teaspoon salt
1 teaspoon dry mustard
1 teaspoon paprika
½ teaspoon curry powder

13 Chicken Both Potted and Stewed

This chapter heading may sound like an invitation to Carry Nation to start her crusade again, hatchet in hand. In truth, it merely eulogizes two more wonderful methods of propelling our feathered friends to greater glory.

CHICKEN-IN-A-POT

1 three-pound stewing chicken, disjointed
1 one-pound can whole tomatoes, undrained
1 cup minced onion
½ cup finely chopped celery
2 teaspoons salt
¼ teaspoon freshly ground pepper
⅛ teaspoon dried thyme
1 bay leaf
1 eleven-ounce can whole-kernel corn, drained
1 eleven-ounce can lima beans, drained
1 eleven-ounce can small, whole potatoes, drained
1 eleven-ounce can peas and carrots, drained

In a large, deep pot combine the chicken, undrained tomatoes, onion, celery, salt, pepper, and herbs. Add water just to cover and simmer, covered, for about 2 hours, or until the chicken is fork tender. Cool the chicken in the broth, then remove the meat from the bones and cut into bite-sized pieces. Return the meat to the pot, first discarding the bay leaf. Add the vegetables and heat, covered. Serve in large soup bowls with hot French bread. (*Serves 6*)

POTTED CHICKEN

1 clove garlic, minced
1 onion, sliced thick
2 thick lemon slices
1 four-pound roasting chicken
3 tablespoons plus 2 teaspoons butter
½ cup chicken broth or stock
¼ pound salt pork, diced
½ pound mushrooms, sliced
1 teaspoon granulated sugar
½ cup dry white wine
1 bay leaf
6 sprigs fresh parsley
2 stalks celery
1 teaspoon salt
¼ teaspoon freshly ground pepper
1 dozen small white onions
1½ cups cooked peas

Place the garlic, onion slices, and lemon slices in the cavity of the chicken. Truss as for roasting, then rub with the 3 tablespoons butter. Brown the chicken thoroughly in a hot Dutch oven, turning on all sides. Add ¼ cup of the chicken broth and set aside.

In a skillet, sauté the salt pork until golden, then remove with a slotted spoon and set aside. In the fat remaining, sauté the mushrooms. Add the remaining ¼ cup chicken broth, the 2 teaspoons butter, and the sugar. Cook until the liquid is reduced by half, then add the reserved salt pork, wine, bay leaf, parsley, celery, salt, and pepper. Stir thoroughly to get up all the little bits, then add all the contents of the skillet to the chicken.

Simmer, covered, about 30 minutes, then add the small white onions and continue cooking, covered, about 10 minutes, or until the chicken is tender. Remove the bay leaf, parsley, and celery. Add the peas and cook until they have heated through, then serve the chicken on a heated platter, surrounded by the vegetables. (*Serves 4*)

POTTED CHICKEN ROAST

5 day-old bread slices, cubed
1 small apple, diced
2 small onions, minced
½ teaspoon salt
½ teaspoon poultry seasoning
¼ cup melted butter
¼ cup hot water
1 four-pound roasting chicken
3 tablespoons butter, more if necessary
1 clove garlic, minced
1 teaspoon dried savory
1 cup sliced mushrooms
1 ten-ounce package frozen green beans, thawed just enough to separate

In a large bowl, combine the bread cubes, apple, onions, salt, poultry seasoning, the melted butter, and 2 tablespoons of the hot water. Lightly stuff the chicken with mixture. Rub the skin of bird with the 3 tablespoons butter and truss as for roasting.

Brown the chicken well on all sides in a hot Dutch oven, (this should take about 25 minutes), adding more butter if necessary. Add the garlic, savory, and remaining 2 tablespoons water and simmer, covered, for 1½ to 2 hours, or until almost tender. Add the mushrooms and beans and continue simmering, covered, another 15 or 20 minutes, or until the beans are tender. Serve the chicken on a heated platter, surrounded by the vegetables. (*Serves 6*)

CHICKEN-IN-THE-POT HENRI IV

2 pounds lean beef
1 marrow bone
1 four-pound chicken, giblets reserved
3 quarts water
½ head white cabbage
2 teaspoons salt
3 carrots, peeled and quartered
2 turnips, peeled and quartered
3 leeks, white part only, chopped
1 celery heart, sliced
2 bay leaves
6 sprigs parsley
1 sprig fresh thyme
6 peppercorns, cracked
1 clove garlic, put through a press

Place the meat, marrow bone, chicken, and water in a deep soup pot and bring slowly to a boil. Skim carefully, then reduce the heat and simmer, covered, for 1 hour.

Meanwhile, cover the cabbage with boiling water and set aside to cool. Skim the stock again, then add the remaining ingredients, including the drained cabbage but excepting the reserved giblets, and simmer for an additional hour. Add the giblets and simmer for 1 hour more. Correct the seasoning, then skin the chicken and serve it whole on a bed of parsley, surrounded by the vegetables. (*Serves 6*)

STUFFED, POT-ROASTED CHICKEN

1 onion, diced
½ cup diced celery
3 tablespoons butter
1¼ cups matzo meal
2 tablespoons chopped fresh parsley
1 teaspoon salt
1½ cups very rich chicken stock, more if necessary
1 egg, lightly beaten
1 four-and-one-half- to five-pound roasting chicken
4 potatoes, peeled and parboiled
4 carrots, peeled, sliced, and parboiled
8 small white onions, peeled and parboiled
1 teaspoon paprika
¼ teaspoon garlic powder
Pepper to taste

Sauté the onion and celery in 1½ tablespoons of the butter until tender, then combine with the matzo meal, parsley, and ½ teaspoon of the salt. Mix half the stock with the egg and add to the matzo meal mixture, then stuff the chicken loosely with the mixture and truss.

Heat the remaining butter in a Dutch oven and brown the chicken on all sides. Pour off the fat, then add the remaining stock. Cover and simmer for 1 hour, breast side up, then add the vegetables, paprika, garlic powder, and remaining ½ teaspoon salt and pepper; simmer, covered, another hour, or until the chicken is fork tender. Add a little more stock, if necessary. (*Serves 6*)

CHICKEN STEW WITH DUMPLINGS

- 1 three-pound stewing chicken, disjointed
- Salt and freshly ground pepper to taste
- 2 tablespoons butter
- ½ cup water
- 1 cup sliced onion
- ¼ teaspoon poultry seasoning
- 1 ten-and-one-half-ounce can condensed cream of chicken soup, undiluted
- 1 ten-ounce package frozen mixed vegetables
- 1 cup packaged biscuit mix
- ⅓ cup whole milk

Sprinkle the chicken generously with salt and pepper, then brown in the butter in a Dutch oven. Add the water, onion, and poultry seasoning. Cover and simmer for 30 minutes, then stir in the soup and vegetables. Bring to a boil, cover again, and simmer another 10 minutes, stirring occasionally.

Make a batter with the biscuit mix and milk, then add by spoonfuls to the hot stew. Cook, uncovered, for 10 minutes, then cover and cook an additional 10 minutes. (*Serves 4*)

BRUNSWICK STEW

- 1 four-pound stewing chicken, disjointed
- 2 quarts water
- Salt
- ½ cup catsup
- 2 teaspoons Worcestershire sauce
- ½ teaspoon Louisiana hot sauce or Tabasco
- 3 tablespoons butter
- Grated rind and juice of ½ lemon
- 4 cups shelled, fresh baby lima beans

4 cups fresh whole-kernel corn
2 cups ½-inch-thick slices fresh okra
4 stalks celery, cut into ½-inch slices
4 cloves garlic, put through a press
2 medium onions, minced
Freshly ground pepper to taste

Combine the chicken, water, and 2 teaspoons salt in a Dutch oven. Simmer, covered, until the chicken is tender (about 3 or 4 hours), then remove the chicken pieces and cool quickly. When cool enough to handle, skin and bone the chicken, cutting the meat into bite-sized pieces. Return the meat to the cooking stock, along with salt to taste and the remaining ingredients. Cover and simmer, stirring occasionally, until the mixture is thick. (*Serves 8*)

CHICKEN STEW MITTEL EUROPA

2 three-pound fryers, disjointed
Salt and freshly ground pepper to taste
1 clove garlic, put through a press
3 onions, sliced thin
3 tablespoons sweet butter
⅛ teaspoon monosodium glutamate
½ cup dry white wine
½ cup water
2 cups sour cream
1 cup chopped ripe olives

Season the chicken with salt and pepper and set aside. Sauté the garlic and sliced onions in the butter, then add the chicken and brown on both sides. Add the monosodium glutamate, wine, and water. Taste for seasoning, then cover and simmer for 1 hour. Stir in the sour cream and olives and simmer *very gently* (or the sour cream will curdle) for another 20 minutes. Serve with a steaming bowl of rice or noodles. (*Serves 6 to 8*)

CHICKEN STEW WITH OKRA

8 slices bacon
½ cup chopped onion
1 large clove garlic, put through a press
2 cups sliced fresh mushrooms
1 three-pound fryer, disjointed
⅓ cup chicken broth
3 tablespoons dry white wine
½ cup heavy cream
1 teaspoon curry powder
1 teaspoon salt
2 medium tomatoes, peeled and chopped
½ pound fresh okra, washed and trimmed

Fry the bacon in a skillet until crisp, then crumble and set aside. Pour off all but 2 tablespoons of the bacon fat and set aside. Sauté onion in the bacon fat in the skillet, then add the garlic and mushrooms and cook until just tender. Remove from pan and reserve. Add another tablespoon of the fat and lightly brown the chicken pieces on both sides. Return the sautéed vegetables to the pan and add the broth, wine, cream, and curry powder. Cover and simmer for 25 minutes, or until the chicken is almost tender, then add the salt, tomatoes, and okra and cook, covered, for 10 minutes longer.

Remove the chicken and vegetables to a serving dish and boil the liquid, uncovered, over high heat until slightly reduced. Pour the liquid over the chicken and garnish with the reserved, crumbled bacon. Steamed rice is an excellent accompaniment. (*Serves 4*)

OLIVE CHICKEN STEW

1 cup chicken stock
1 cup chopped onion
1 cup chopped celery
3 cups sliced carrots
½ cup sliced, stuffed green olives
1½ cups milk
2 cups grated sharp Cheddar or Tillamook cheese
1 teaspoon Worcestershire sauce
Pinch of cayenne
2 cups diced, cooked chicken

Combine the chicken stock and all the vegetables except the olives, cover, and cook until the vegetables are tender. Add the remaining ingredients, mixing well, and cook over medium heat, stirring constantly, until the cheese is melted. (*Serves 6*)

SIMPLE CHICKEN STEW

4 whole peppercorns
1 whole clove
1 small carrot, sliced
1 small onion, sliced
2 stalks celery, leaves and all, sliced diagonally
1 four-pound chicken, disjointed
1 teaspoon salt
2 tablespoons all-purpose flour (optional)

Tie the peppercorns, whole clove, and vegetables in cheesecloth and place in a deep kettle with the chicken. Cover the chicken with water, cover, and simmer until tender, adding the salt about halfway through the process (about 1 hour). Remove the seasonings and chicken and boil the stock down to about 2 cups. (If you like your gravy thickish, mix a little cold water with about 2 tablespoons flour and add to the hot stock very gradually, stirring constantly, and cook until thickened.) Return the chicken to the boiling gravy and taste for seasoning. (*Serves 8*)

Note: This is delicious served over rice or noodles.

GINGERED CHICKEN STEW

1 three-pound fryer, disjointed
3 tablespoons peanut oil
2 large onions, chopped
1 clove garlic, put through a press
1½ cups chicken broth
3 slices fresh ginger
1 bay leaf
1 cup catsup
1 cup chunked green pepper
½ cup raisins
¼ cup toasted, slivered almonds

Brown the chicken pieces in the peanut oil, along with the onion and garlic. Add 1 cup of the broth, the ginger, and bay leaf. Bring to a boil, then reduce the heat and simmer for 30 minutes. Mix the catsup with the remaining broth and stir into the pan liquid. Add the green pepper and raisins, cover, and simmer for 15 minutes. Just before serving, sprinkle with the almonds. (*Serves 4 to 6*)

CHICKEN STEW, SPANISH STYLE

- 1 five-pound chicken, disjointed
- Salt and freshly ground pepper
- All-purpose flour
- ¼ cup (½ stick) butter
- 2 onions, sliced
- 1 cup chopped green olives
- 1 green pepper, chopped
- 2 cups chopped fresh tomatoes
- 1 teaspoon granulated sugar
- 2 cups peas
- 1 cup sliced mushrooms

Season the chicken well with salt and pepper and dredge with flour. Brown on both sides in the butter, then remove from the pan. Cook the onions, olives, green pepper, tomatoes, and the sugar in the same fat for 10 minutes. Add the chicken and enough water to cover and simmer, closely covered, for about 1½ hours, or until the chicken is tender. Add the peas, mushrooms, and 2 teaspoons salt. Combine 2 tablespoons flour with a little cold water, mix until smooth, and stir gradually into the hot stew. Cover and cook another 20 minutes. (*Serves 8 to 10*)

CHICKEN STEW AUSTRIAN

- 1 onion, chopped
- 4 slices bacon
- 2 three-pound fryers, disjointed
- 1 teaspoon all-purpose flour
- 1 clove garlic, put through a press
- 1½ cups white wine
- 1 quart chicken stock
- 1 teaspoon paprika
- Salt and freshly ground pepper
- ½ cup sour cream

Cook the onion and bacon for 2 to 3 minutes in a Dutch oven. Add the chicken and sauté until golden brown on both sides, then remove and stir the flour into the fat remaining in the pot. Add the garlic, stir, and cook for 2 minutes, then add the wine, chicken stock, paprika, salt, and pepper. Return the chicken to the pot, cover, and cook gently for about 30 minutes, or until the chicken is fork tender. Add the sour cream slowly, stirring until the gravy is very smooth. (Do not boil.) Serve with hot noodles. (*Serves 6 to 8*)

WHOLE STEWED CHICKEN

1 five-pound young roasting chicken
Salt and freshly ground pepper
1 cup whole oysters
1 tablespoon butter
1 tablespoon all-purpose flour
⅛ teaspoon dried oregano
⅔ cup half-and-half
4 hard-cooked eggs, chopped fine

Season the chicken inside and out with salt and pepper, then stuff the cavity with the oysters and close the opening with skewers. Truss as for roasting. Cook in a pressure cooker, following manufacturer's directions for proper timing.

In the meantime, melt the butter in a saucepan and blend in the flour and oregano. Cook, stirring, until the mixture bubbles. When the chicken is done, add the liquid from pressure cooker plus the half-and-half, stirring constantly. Taste for seasoning, then add the chopped eggs. Let the mixture come to a gentle boil, pour over the chicken, and serve at once. (*Serves 6*)

14 Fricassees

Gammy's Favorites

I generally equate chicken fricassee with the old plantation, hoopskirts, and a faithful family retainer bearing silver platters of chicken studded with dumplings roughly the size of magnolia blossoms. None of these is my heritage—unless I fudge a little about the location of the Mason-Dixon line. Our home was no white-pillared Tara, and the beloved family retainer was my own warm, wonderful Czech mother, "Gammy," who cooked rings around everybody else's mom, fricassee included, and ethnic background be hanged.

(I grudgingly admit I was well over twenty-one before I learned that fricassee was born in France and *not* the Deep South! I still don't know about the dumplings.)

GAMMY'S CHICKEN FRICASSEE WITH CORN DUMPLINGS

1 five-pound stewing chicken, disjointed
Salt and freshly ground pepper to taste
½ cup all-purpose flour
⅓ cup butter
2 carrots, peeled and diced

2 stalks celery, leaves and all, sliced
1 large onion, chopped
¼ teaspoon dried marjoram
½ small bay leaf
½ teaspoon garlic powder
Gammy's Corn Dumplings (see below)

Season the chicken with salt and pepper and dredge with the flour, then brown well in the melted butter in a large skillet. When browned, transfer to a Dutch oven.

Rinse out the skillet with hot water, scrape up all the crunchy bits, and pour into the Dutch oven to a depth of 1½ inches. Add the carrots, celery, onion, 1 teaspoon salt, and the spices then cover tightly, and simmer very slowly for about 2 hours, or until the chicken is fork tender.

Serve with the dumplings. (*Serves 6*)

GAMMY'S CORN DUMPLINGS

1 cup stone-ground cornmeal
1 teaspoon salt
2 cups boiling water
¾ cup plus 1 tablespoon all-purpose flour
2½ teaspoons baking powder
Freshly ground pepper
1 whole egg
¾ cup cooked or canned whole-kernel corn
2 tablespoons melted butter
1 teaspoon minced onion

Add the cornmeal and salt slowly to the boiling water. Cook, stirring constantly, for 2 minutes, then remove from the heat and cool. Sift the ¾ cup flour, baking powder, and pepper, then sift again and remeasure. Stir into the cornmeal mixture. Beat the egg lightly and add to the flour-cornmeal mixture, then chop the corn and add to the mixture, along with the butter and onion. Roll into balls, then roll the balls in the 1 tablespoon flour. Drop the dumplings on top of the chicken and cook, covered, for 15 minutes.

CREOLE CHICKEN FRICASSEE

¼ cup (½ stick) butter
1 five-pound stewing chicken, disjointed
¼ cup all-purpose flour
2 cups water
1 large onion, chopped
6 fresh tomatoes (or equivalent in canned tomatoes), chopped
3 tablespoons chopped fresh parsley
Salt and freshly ground pepper to taste

Heat the butter in a heavy skillet and brown the chicken pieces, then transfer to a Dutch oven. Carefully stir the flour into the drippings in the skillet so it doesn't lump. Slowly add the water, stirring constantly until the gravy is smooth and bubbling hot, then pour over the chicken. Add the remaining ingredients, cover tightly, and cook over low heat for 1½ hours, or until the chicken is very tender. Serve with hot rice. (*Serves 4 to 6*)

VERMICELLI FRICASSEE

1 four- to five-pound stewing chicken, disjointed
3 cups canned tomatoes
2 onions, chopped
3 green peppers, sliced thin
2 cloves garlic, put through a press
½ pound vermicelli
Salt and freshly ground pepper to taste
Butter
½ cup freshly grated Parmesan cheese

Put the chicken parts into a stewing pot or Dutch oven and cover with boiling water. Simmer for about 1 hour, or until the chicken is almost done.

Add the tomatoes, onion, green peppers, and garlic and cook an additional 25 minutes, then add the vermicelli, salt, and pepper and bring to a gentle boil. Boil only until vermicelli is done (read the package directions, as timing varies with each brand). Turn into a baking dish, dot with butter, and cover thickly with grated Parmesan cheese. Brown for 20 minutes in a 350° oven. (*Serves 4 to 6*)

CHICKEN-LOBSTER FRICASSEE

1 five-pound young roasting chicken
Salt and freshly ground pepper to taste
5 cups water
1½ cups dry vermouth or other white wine
2 bay leaves
¼ teaspoon dried oregano
Juice of 1 lime
1 large onion, cut in eighths
1½ tablespoons arrowroot
3 cups hot, cooked rice
3 lobster tails, cooked, cut in chunks, and kept hot
Minced fresh parsley for garnish

Season the cavity of the chicken with salt and pepper and truss as for roasting. Place the chicken in a Dutch oven and pour the water and vermouth over it. Add the bay leaves, oregano, lime juice, and onion and bring to a boil. Reduce the heat, cover tightly, and simmer for about 2 hours, or until the chicken is tender, then remove the bird from the broth and cool. When able to handle, skin and remove the bones, but leave the chicken meat in large pieces.

Strain 4 cups of the broth into a saucepan. Mix the arrowroot with a little cold water, then place the saucepan over low heat and slowly add the arrowroot water, stirring constantly until the mixture thickens.

Mound the hot rice on a heated platter (a good, deep one), arrange the chicken and lobster meat on top, and pour the hot sauce over all. Sprinkle with minced parsley and serve at once. (*Serves 6*)

MARY TODD'S FRICASSEE

¼ cup (½ stick) butter
1 four-pound chicken, disjointed
2 cups half-and-half
Salt and freshly ground pepper to taste
¼ teaspoon ground mace
¼ teaspoon freshly grated nutmeg
1 cup cooked, puréed onions
Scant 1 tablespoon arrowroot
20 green asparagus tips, fresh cooked or canned

Heat the butter in a skillet and brown the chicken on all sides, then cover the skillet and simmer until the chicken is tender (about 50 minutes). Remove and keep hot on a deep serving platter. Skim off some of the fat in the pan and slowly add the half-and-half, stirring constantly. Season the mixture well with salt, pepper, mace, and nutmeg, then add the puréed onions and stir again.

Blend together the arrowroot and a little cold water and gradually combine with the cream sauce; blend until it reaches the proper consistency (not *too* thick). Bring just to a boil, then remove from the heat, add the asparagus tips, and pour immediately over the chicken. (*Serves 4*)

CHICKEN FRICASSEE WITH VEGETABLES

¾ cup all-purpose flour
Salt and white pepper to taste
2 two-and-one-half-pound chickens, quartered
¼ cup (½ stick) butter
2 cups chicken broth
3 tablespoons minced fresh parsley
1 one-pound can small white onions, drained
1 ten-ounce package frozen peas, thawed
⅔ cup dry vermouth or white wine
2 cups half-and-half
⅛ teaspoon ground mace
⅛ teaspoon freshly grated nutmeg

Combine ¼ cup of the flour with salt and pepper and dredge the chicken in the mixture, then heat the butter in a Dutch oven and brown the chicken on both sides. Pour the broth around the fowl and sprinkle with the parsley, then cover tightly and bake in a 350° oven for about 1 hour. When the hour is up, place the onions around the chicken and distribute the peas over both. Cover again and continue baking another 10 minutes, or until the peas are cooked through. Remove the chicken and vegetables to a tureen and keep hot.

Remove the fat from the broth in the Dutch oven. Make a thin paste of the remaining flour and vermouth and add to the broth, then heat on top of the stove, stirring constantly. Slowly add the half-and-half and simmer, stirring, until the mixture thickens. Season well with mace and nutmeg, adding more salt and pepper if necessary. Pour the gravy over the chicken in the tureen and serve with small biscuits. (*Serves 6 to 8*)

CURRIED FRICASSEE

2 two-pound fryers, disjointed and skinned
1 large onion, minced
3 tablespoons butter
Salt and freshly ground pepper to taste
2 tablespoons curry powder
Chicken broth
8 sprigs fresh parsley
1 bay leaf
Pinch of dried thyme
1 apple, chopped
½ cup condensed cream of mushroom soup, undiluted
3 egg yolks, beaten
Hot, cooked rice

Brown the chicken and onion lightly in the butter, then add salt, pepper, and the curry powder. Add broth just to cover, along with the parsley, bay leaf, thyme, and apple. Cover and simmer until the chicken is tender (about 1 hour), then remove to a hot platter.

Blend the soup with a little of the warm gravy from the pan. Add the beaten egg yolks, stir gradually into the gravy, and cook until thickened, then simmer 2 to 3 minutes longer, being careful not to boil.

Make a flattish mound of hot, cooked rice on a serving platter. Arrange the chicken parts on the rice and pour the gravy over all. (*Serves 6*)

OLD-TIME FRICASSEE

Chicken

- **1 five- to six-pound stewing chicken, disjointed**
- **1 large onion, sliced**
- **2 large stalks celery, leaves and all, sliced**
- **1 tablespoon salt**
- **Freshly ground pepper to taste**
- **2½ cups water**
- **Chicken broth, if necessary**
- **¼ cup all-purpose flour**

Red Country Dumplings

- **2 cups sifted all-purpose flour**
- **1 tablespoon baking powder**
- **1 teaspoon salt**
- **¼ teaspoon paprika**
- **2 tablespoons shortening**
- **1 cup milk**

Place the chicken, onion, celery, salt, pepper, and 2 cups of the water in a Dutch oven. Cover and simmer for 1½ hours, or until the chicken is tender. Allow the chicken to cool in the broth, then skin and bone the chicken parts, leaving the meat in as large pieces as possible.

Strain the broth into a quart measure, adding extra broth, if necessary, to make up the quart. (Use your freezer stock, a can of chicken broth, or—*in extremis*—a chicken bouillon cube dissolved in boiling water.) Put the vegetables through a food mill or strainer and return the pulp to the broth. Heat to boiling. Stir the flour into the remaining ½ cup cold water, then carefully blend the mixture into the hot broth. Cook, stirring constantly, until the gravy thickens, then boil for an additional minute. Return the chicken to the pot and heat slowly while you prepare the dumplings.

Sift together the flour, baking powder, salt, and paprika. Cut in the shortening until the mixture is crumbly. Stir in the milk just until the mixture is moistened, then drop the batter in about 6 mounds on top of the chicken. Cook, tightly covered, for 20 minutes. (*Serves 6*)

BROWN CHICKEN FRICASSEE

3 small slices salt pork, diced
1 three-pound chicken, disjointed
2 tablespoons all-purpose flour
2 cups boiling chicken broth
Salt and freshly ground pepper to taste
1½ teaspoons onion juice

Render the salt pork in a skillet, and when it sizzles add the chicken parts and brown to a deep, rich golden color. Remove the chicken and keep warm.

Add the flour to the fat in the skillet and stir to make a thick roux. Cook for 2 minutes. Add the boiling chicken broth and stir constantly until smooth, then return the chicken to the skillet and season to taste with salt and pepper. Cover the skillet and simmer gently until the chicken is tender (about 50 minutes), then add the onion juice and stir to blend it into the gravy. Serve at once with tiny dumplings. (*Serves 4*)

JAMAICAN CHICKEN FRICASSEE

1 tablespoon butter
2 tablespoons light brown sugar
1 three-and-one-half-pound chicken, disjointed
2 onions, chopped
1 tablespoon wine vinegar
2 teaspoons salt
1 teaspoon freshly ground pepper
1 bay leaf

- ½ teaspoon dried thyme
- 1 four-and-one-half-ounce can button mushrooms
- 1 one-pound can stewed tomatoes
- 1 tablespoon all-purpose flour

Melt the butter in a large, heavy skillet. Add the brown sugar and heat until the sugar melts and bubbles, then brown the chicken on both sides. Add the onions and cook until transparent. Stir in the vinegar, salt, pepper, herbs, mushrooms, and tomatoes, then cover and simmer about 30 minutes, or until the chicken is tender. Thicken the sauce with the flour dissolved in a little cold water and serve very hot. *(Serves 6)*

FRICASSEE ON THE HOT SIDE

- 1 four-pound chicken, disjointed
- 3 large onions, sliced
- 2 cups hot water
- 1¾ cups tomato juice
- ¼ teaspoon cayenne
- 3 teaspoons salt
- ¼ teaspoon black pepper
- ¼ teaspoon dry mustard
- 5 teaspoons Worcestershire sauce
- 2 small bay leaves
- Scant 1 teaspoon granulated sugar
- 3 cloves garlic, put through a press

Put the chicken pieces in the bottom of a Dutch oven and cover with the sliced onions. Pour in the water, cover, and simmer for about 1 hour, or until the chicken is nearly done, turning the pieces occasionally. Combine the tomato juice with the remaining ingredients in a saucepan. Bring to a boil, then lower the heat and simmer for 10 minutes. Pour off all but ¾ cup of liquid from the chicken pot and add the spiced tomato juice. Cover and bake in a 350° oven for 30 minutes, basting occasionally. *(Serves 6)*

15 Chicken Pies

Some of the commercially made chicken pies that crowd your grocer's bountiful freezer are very good indeed, but not one can claim to be as succulent, as deeply soul-satisfying, as the chicken-rich pies baked by loving hands at home.

GAMMY'S CHICKEN PIE

I have taken liberties with my mother's recipe simply because I have to measure, not being adept at cooking by "feel" like Gammy and others of her generation. I also like the appearance and texture of vegetables prepared with a small ball cutter.

Pastry Topping

1 cup sifted all-purpose flour
½ teaspoon salt
1 teaspoon baking powder
½ cup shortening, well chilled
¼ cup ice water
1 egg white
A little light cream or half-and-half

Filling

- **1 four-pound stewing chicken, cooked, boned, and diced**
- **12 tiny white onions, cooked**
- **1 cup cooked potato balls**
- **½ cup button mushrooms**
- **½ cup cooked carrot balls**
- **½ cup cooked peas**
- **2 hard-cooked eggs, quartered**
- **Salt and freshly ground pepper to taste**
- **Chicken stock, mixed with ½ cup cream and thickened with a little flour**

Prepare the pastry first. Sift the dry ingredients together. Add the chilled shortening, cutting it in with a pastry blender or 2 knives until the dough resembles cornmeal. Add the ice water, a couple of tablespoonfuls at a time, blending it in *lightly* and handling as little as possible. When the dough forms a ball it is ready to be chilled for a couple of hours.

Meanwhile combine the solid ingredients for the filling and season generously with salt and pepper. Place in a large, deep casserole and pour in enough of the thickened chicken stock/cream mixture just to cover. Allow the flavors to meld while you roll out the crust.

Roll the chilled dough out on a lightly floured board. Brush with egg white and drape the dough, egg-white side down, over the top of the casserole. Fold the edges back over themselves and crimp the edges neatly. Slash the dough in several places, then bake in a preheated 475° oven for 8 to 10 minutes. At that point brush the pastry top with a little light cream, then lower the heat to 350° and bake another 20 to 25 minutes. (*Serves 8*)

CHICKEN PIE, COTTAGE STYLE

- 1 ten-and-one-half-ounce can cream of chicken soup, undiluted
- ¼ cup chicken broth or stock
- 2 cups diced, cooked chicken
- ½ cup diced celery
- 1 ten-ounce package frozen peas
- ¼ cup diced pimiento
- 1¼ teaspoons salt
- ¾ teaspoon poultry seasoning
- Garlic powder to taste
- 2 hard-cooked eggs, diced
- 1 envelope instant mashed potatoes
- 1 whole raw egg, separated
- ¼ teaspoon salt

Combine all the ingredients except the instant mashed potatoes, raw egg, and salt in a 2-quart casserole and set aside. Prepare the potatoes according to package directions, and beat in the egg yolk. Add the salt to the egg white and beat until stiff. Fold into the potatoes, then spread the mixture over the top of the casserole. Bake in a 375° oven for 30 minutes, or until potato "crust" is golden brown. (*Serves 6*)

COCK-A-LEEKIE PIE

- 1 four- to five-pound roasting chicken, disjointed
- 2 cups plus 3 tablespoons cold water
- 1 large onion, quartered
- ½ stalk celery
- 3 sprigs fresh parsley

2 small bay leaves
½ teaspoon dried thyme
Salt
5 whole black peppercorns
8 leeks
¼ pound tongue, cooked and sliced
1 tablespoon minced fresh parsley
2½ tablespoons all-purpose flour
Pastry for a 1-crust pie
¼ cup heavy cream

Place the chicken in a large kettle, along with the 2 cups water, onion, celery, parsley sprigs, bay leaves, thyme, about 2½ teaspoons salt, and the peppercorns. Bring to a boil, then reduce the heat and simmer, covered, about 1½ hours, or until fork tender.

Meanwhile, trim the root ends and tops of the leeks and cut into 1-inch pieces. Cook in boiling salted water about 5 minutes, then drain.

When the chicken is done, remove from the broth and continue cooking the broth for 5 minutes. Place the chicken parts (breasts boned and cut into 4 nice pieces) in an oblong, 2-inch-deep baking dish. Place the drained leeks on top of the chicken, then add the tongue and sprinkle with chopped parsley. Mix the flour with the 3 tablespoons cold water and place in a small saucepan. Slowly stir in 2 cups of the strained chicken broth. Bring to a boil, stirring constantly, and pour over the ingredients in the baking dish.

Top the baking dish with your favorite pastry, crimping the edges and leaving a small steam hole in the center. Bake in a 425° oven for about 35 minutes, or until the crust is golden brown. Place the pie on a cake rack. Heat the cream and pour through the center hole in the pastry. Allow the pie to "rest" about 10 minutes, then serve. (*Serves 6 to 8*)

ANNIE'S CHICKEN PIE

1/4 cup (1/2 stick) butter
1/2 cup all-purpose flour
3 cups chicken broth
1/2 cup half-and-half
Milk
1/2 teaspoon ground ginger
Salt and freshly ground pepper to taste
1 three-and-one-half-pound stewing chicken, cooked and boned
2 hard-cooked eggs, sliced
1 cup packaged biscuit mix

Melt the butter in a saucepan and blend in the flour. Combine the broth, cream, and 1/2 cup milk and add all at once. Cook, stirring constantly, until smooth and thickened. Add ginger, salt, and pepper and cook a minute or two longer, then taste for seasoning.

Arrange the chicken in a shallow baking dish. Lay the sliced eggs on top, then pour the sauce over all. Combine 1/4 cup milk with the biscuit mix, then roll out the biscuit dough to a thickness of 1/4 inch on a floured board. Trim to fit the baking dish with an overhang of about 1/2 inch. Cut steam vents, then place the dough over chicken and flute the edges, pressing to the edges of the baking dish. Brush the pastry with milk and bake at 425° for 20 to 25 minutes, or until the top is browned and the sauce bubbles. Cool for 5 to 10 minutes before serving. (*Serves 4 to 6*)

CHICKEN PIE MEXICALI

Pastry for a 2-crust pie
4 slices bacon, diced
1 small onion, diced
2 tomatoes, chopped
½ teaspoon oregano
1 teaspoon salt
1 pimiento, chopped
1½ cups diced, cooked chicken
1 tablespoon chopped fresh parsley
½ cup pitted, halved ripe olives
¼ cup raisins
1 tablespoon all-purpose flour

Roll out half the pastry and use it to line a greased baking dish (about 10 x 6 x 2 inches). Set aside. Cook together the bacon and onion until the bacon is *just* browned, then add the tomatoes, oregano, salt, pimiento, and chicken. Simmer for 15 minutes, stirring frequently, then add the parsley, olives, raisins, and flour. Place the mixture in the pastry-lined baking dish and cover with the pastry top, rolled ¼ inch thick. Make a series of vents in the pastry, then bake in a 375° oven for 20 to 25 minutes. (*Serves 6*)

TOPSY-TURVY PIE

Chicken

1 two-and-one-half-pound chicken, disjointed
Seasoned all-purpose flour
½ cup (1 stick) butter
½ cup sliced, stuffed olives

Corn Batter

1½ cups yellow cornmeal
½ cup sifted all-purpose flour
3½ teaspoons baking powder
1 tablespoon granulated sugar
2 tablespoons shortening
2 eggs, lightly beaten
1 cup whole milk

Chicken Gravy

¼ cup all-purpose flour
¼ cup reserved fat from the fried chicken
2½ cups chicken broth, milk, or water
Salt and freshly ground pepper to taste

Dredge the chicken in flour seasoned with salt and pepper and fry in very hot butter until fork tender. Drain and reserve the fat. Arrange chicken parts in a casserole and fill in the spaces with the stuffed olives. Set aside while you prepare the corn batter.

Sift the dry ingredients together, then cut in the shortening until the mixture resembles tiny peas. Combine the eggs and milk and add to dry ingredients, stirring just enough to combine. Cover the chicken-olive mixture with the batter and bake at 425° for 25 to 30 minutes.

Meanwhile, make the gravy. Blend the flour into the fat over low heat and cook slowly, stirring constantly, until it bubbles. Add the liquid very gradually, then add the salt and pepper, stirring constantly until the gravy is thick and rich.

When the chicken is done, invert it onto a warm platter. Pass the gravy separately. (*Serves 4 to 6*)

INDIVIDUAL CHICKEN PIES PARISIENNE

1 four-pound stewing chicken
2½ teaspoons salt
1 large carrot
1 onion
Bouquet garni (parsley sprigs, large bay leaf, celery stalk with leaves, and sprig of fresh thyme, tied loosely in a square of cheesecloth)
½ cup mushrooms
2 tablespoons butter
¼ cup all-purpose flour
¼ teaspoon freshly ground pepper
¼ teaspoon freshly grated nutmeg
1 cup chicken stock
½ cup dry sherry
Pastry for a 2-crust pie
6 slices boiled ham
1 egg yolk, beaten with 2 tablespoons water
½ cup half-and-half
2 tablespoons chopped fresh parsley

Place the chicken in a large kettle, cover with water, and add 2 teaspoons of the salt, the carrot, onion, and bouquet garni. Cover and simmer until tender (about 2 to 2½ hours), then remove chicken from broth and cool.

Slice the mushrooms and sauté in butter for 4 minutes, then remove the mushrooms and blend the flour, remaining salt, the pepper, and nutmeg into the juices in the pan. Add the cup of stock and continue cooking, stirring, until the sauce is thick and smooth. Put mushrooms back into the pan and add the sherry, stirring constantly. Cook until smooth. Set aside.

On a lightly floured board, roll the pastry out into a 12 x 16-inch rectangle. Cut into 12 four-inch squares. Cut the chicken from the bone in as large slices as possible, discarding the skin. Place a slice of chicken and a slice of ham on each of 6 pastry squares, then spoon 2 tablespoons of the sauce over each. Brush the edges of the pastry with the egg yolk–water mixture. Top with the remaining pastry squares and seal the edges together by pressing with the fingers. Cut a small vent in the top of each pastry, brush with the remaining egg yolk–water mixture, and place on a greased baking sheet. Bake in a 400° oven for 15 minutes, or until brown.

Meanwhile, thin the remaining sauce with half-and-half, taste for seasoning, and heat thoroughly. Sprinkle with parsley and serve at table in a sauceboat. (*Serves 6*)

CURRIED CHICKEN PIE

2 tablespoons butter
1 tablespoon all-purpose flour
1¼ teaspoons curry powder
1 ten-and-one-half-ounce can chicken gravy
½ cup sliced mushrooms
½ cup cooked peas
1½ cups diced, cooked chicken
Salt and pepper to taste
2 tablespoons dry sherry
1 package instant mashed potatoes

Melt the butter in a large saucepan, then stir in the flour and curry powder. Blend in the chicken gravy and cook, stirring constantly, until thickened. Stir in the mushrooms, peas, chicken, seasonings, and sherry, then turn the mixture into a shallow casserole.

Prepare the potatoes as directed on the package, then press through a pastry tube to form a decorative border, or drop by spoonfuls on top of the casserole contents. Bake at 350° for 20 minutes, or until the potatoes are lightly browned. (*Serves 4*)

MUSHROOM CHICKEN PIE

4 small white onions, sliced thin
1 tablespoon chopped green pepper
2 tablespoons butter
1 ten-and-one-half-ounce can condensed cream of mushroom soup
½ cup milk
1 cup diced, cooked chicken
½ cup diced, cooked carrots or a combination of peas and carrots
1 cup packaged biscuit mix

Cook the onions and green pepper in the butter until soft. Combine with the soup, half the milk, the chicken, and carrots, then pour into an 8-inch pie plate. Add the remaining milk to the biscuit mix to make a dough. Roll the dough into a circle about 9 inches in diameter, place on top of the chicken mixture, and flute the edge. Bake in a 450° oven for 15 minutes. (*Serves 4*)

THREE-IN-ONE CHICKEN PIE

¾ cup (1½ sticks) butter
½ pound mushrooms, sliced
1 tablespoon minced onion
¾ cup all-purpose flour

4½ cups rich chicken broth
1½ cups diced, cooked ham
1 four-and-one-half- to five-pound chicken, cooked, boned, skinned, and diced
Salt and freshly ground pepper to taste
1 cup packaged biscuit mix
¼ cup milk
1 egg, beaten with 2 tablespoons water

Melt the butter in a deep skillet and sauté the mushrooms and onion. Push the mushrooms to one side and add the flour, stirring constantly until the mixture is smooth. Slowly add the chicken broth, stirring, and cook gently until thickened. Add the ham, chicken, salt, and pepper, then pour into a 2-quart casserole.

Combine the biscuit mix with the milk to make a dough. Roll out the dough to a thickness of ¼ inch and place it over the top of the casserole. Cut vents in the dough and crimp the edges; then brush with the egg-water mixture. Bake in a 450° oven until brown and bubbly. (*Serves 6 to 8*)

16 Creamed Chicken

And Other Weighty Problems

Dedicated to the calories-for-lunch bunch and other hip types. For obvious reasons, this is not my favorite section.

OLD RELIABLE (CREAMED CHICKEN)

3 tablespoons butter
3 tablespoons all-purpose flour
1 cup well-seasoned chicken broth
½ cup cream
2 cups large-diced, cooked chicken
1 four-ounce can mushrooms, undrained
Salt and freshly ground pepper to taste
1 tablespoon sherry
6 individual patty shells, toast points, rice, or 6 waffles

Melt the butter in a large saucepan and blend in the flour. Add the chicken broth and cream and stir until thickened and smooth. Add the chicken and mushrooms with their liquid and cook for 1 minute. Season to taste and then stir in the sherry.

Serve in patty shells, on toast points, over rice, or, for a change, over waffles. (*Serves 6*)

KISSIN' COUSIN (CHICKEN À LA KING)

- ¼ cup (½ stick) butter
- ¼ cup all-purpose flour
- 2 cups half-and-half
- 1 egg yolk, lightly beaten
- ½ green pepper, diced
- 1½ cups diced, cooked chicken
- ½ cup halved, blanched almonds
- 1 cup sliced, sautéed mushrooms
- Salt and freshly ground pepper to taste
- 1 cup cooked peas
- 1 four-ounce jar pimientos, sliced
- 2 tablespoons sherry
- 6 individual patty shells, toast points, or 6 English muffins, halved and toasted

Melt the butter in the top of a double boiler over direct heat, then add the flour and blend well. Add the half-and-half gradually, stirring until the sauce is smooth. When it just begins to bubble, reduce heat, add the egg yolk, and stir until thickened. Add all the other ingredients except the sherry and patty shells, mix well, and place over boiling water. Cook until thoroughly heated. Just before serving, stir in the sherry and taste for seasoning.

Serve in patty shells, over toast points, or on toasted English muffin halves. (*Serves 6*)

CHICKEN AND SWEETBREADS IN CREAM

- **1 pair (1 pound) sweetbreads**
- **Salt**
- **1 cup sliced mushrooms**
- **6 tablespoons (¾ stick) butter**
- **¼ cup all-purpose flour**
- **1 cup well-seasoned chicken stock**
- **½ cup cream**
- **1 teaspoon grated onion**
- **Pinch of cayenne**
- **Freshly ground pepper to taste**
- **½ green pepper, cut in strips**
- **¼ cup chopped pimiento**
- **2 cups diced, cooked chicken**
- **2 egg yolks, hard-cooked and sieved**
- **10 small patty shells**

Prepare the sweetbreads by simmering in salted water to cover for 25 minutes. Drain, then rinse under cold water. Slip off the membrane, cut out the dark veins and connective tissues, and cut into cubes. Set aside.

Sauté the mushrooms in 2 tablespoons of the butter until soft. Melt the remaining butter, add the flour, and blend. Add the chicken stock and stir until smooth, then add the cream, grated onion, cayenne, salt, pepper, green pepper, pimiento, sweetbreads, chicken, and mushrooms. Carefully stir in the hard-cooked, sieved egg yolks. Serve at once in individual patty shells. (*Serves 10*)

CHICKEN FOR A JUNE BRIDE

- 6 tablespoons (¾ stick) butter
- ⅓ cup all-purpose flour
- 1 cup well-seasoned chicken broth
- 1 cup heavy cream
- Scant tablespoon salt
- ⅓ teaspoon paprika
- ¼ teaspoon each white pepper, freshly grated nutmeg, and saffron
- ½ pound mushrooms, sliced
- 1 medium onion, chopped fine
- 1 green pepper, cut into very thin strips
- 2 large pimientos, finely chopped
- 3 cups highly seasoned, cooked, chunked chicken meat
- 3 tablespoons lemon juice
- 1 large pastry shell
- Parsley sprigs and pimiento for garnish

In the top of a double boiler, melt 4 tablespoons of the butter over direct heat and stir in the flour. When smooth, add the chicken broth and cream and cook, stirring, until thickened. Season with the salt, paprika, pepper, nutmeg, and saffron, then let cool.

Sauté the vegetables in the remaining butter until the onion is limp and transparent. Drain on paper toweling, then combine with the chicken and sauce. Heat over boiling water. Just before serving, add the lemon juice and mix well.

Serve in a large pastry shell and decorate with parsley sprigs and pimiento cut in fancy shapes. (*Serves 8 to 10*)

CHICKEN GABRIELLE

2 tablespoons butter
2 tablespoons all-purpose flour
½ cup milk
2 cups diced, cooked chicken
½ cup light cream
Pinch of cayenne
½ teaspoon Worcestershire sauce
1 teaspoon salt
1 tablespoon sherry
3 ripe avocados, peeled, halved, and pitted

Melt the butter in a saucepan and stir in the flour. Add the milk and cook, stirring, until thickened and smooth, then add the chicken, cream, cayenne, Worcestershire sauce, and salt. Simmer for 3 minutes, then remove from the heat and stir in the sherry. Pile the mixture into the avocado halves and run under the broiler to brown. (*Serves 6*)

ANGOSTURA CHICKEN

¼ cup (½ stick) butter
1¾ tablespoons all-purpose flour
¾ cup chicken stock
¼ cup thin cream
¼ teaspoon salt
Pinch of freshly ground pepper
1 teaspoon Angostura bitters
1 cup diced, cooked chicken
4 eggs, hard-cooked and cut in eighths
½ cup sautéed, sliced mushrooms
¼ pound almonds, blanched and chopped
1 nine-and-a-half-ounce can Chinese chow mein noodles

Melt the butter in the top of a double boiler over direct heat, then add the flour. Stir in the stock slowly and cook, stirring, until thick and smooth. Add the cream, salt, and pepper and reheat, but do *not* allow to boil. Add all the other ingredients except the noodles, folding them lightly into the sauce, and heat in a double boiler. Serve hot, on a mound of Chinese noodles. (*Serves 4*)

SOUTH SEAS CHICKEN

- **¼ cup butter**
- **¼ cup all-purpose flour**
- **1 teaspoon salt**
- **Pinch of white pepper**
- **1½ cups half-and-half**
- **1 cup chicken broth**
- **2 cups diced, cooked chicken**
- **1 cup pineapple chunks**
- **3 tablespoons shredded coconut**
- **Toast points, rice, or individual patty shells**
- **Chopped parsley for garnish**

Melt the butter in a saucepan. Add the flour, salt, and pepper and stir until smooth. Gradually add the half-and-half and broth, stirring until thick and smooth. Stir in chicken, pineapple, and coconut and heat to just below the boiling point. Serve over toast points, on rice, or in patty shells, sprinkled generously with chopped parsley. (*Serves 4 to 6*)

FLAMING CHICKEN AMANDINE

- **1 four-pound stewing chicken**
- **2 quarts plus 2 tablespoons water**
- **Bouquet garni (parsley sprigs, sprig of fresh thyme, 5 to 6 peppercorns, bay leaf, tied in a piece of cheesecloth)**
- **1 large carrot**

1 onion stuck with 2 cloves
2 egg yolks
1 cup light cream
1 teaspoon granulated sugar
1 teaspoon monosodium glutamate
1½ teaspoons salt
2 tablespoons butter
2 tablespoons all-purpose flour
1 tablespoon minced green pepper
1 tablespoon minced pimiento
½ cup small-diced mushrooms
½ cup sliced, toasted almonds
¼ cup high-proof rum, warmed
Toast points

Cook the chicken in the 2 quarts of water, along with the bouquet garni, carrot, and onion, for about 2 hours, or until tender. Allow the chicken to cool in the broth, then skin, bone, and cut the meat into large dice. Set aside.

Strain the broth and heat 2 cups of it (saving the rest to freeze as stock or to use for another purpose). Meanwhile, beat the egg yolks and blend well with the cream. Slowly add to hot chicken broth, stirring vigorously until smooth. Add the sugar, monosodium glutamate, and salt. Heat to the simmering point. Meantime, melt the 2 tablespoons of butter in a large skillet, then add the flour, stirring until well blended. Add the hot cream-broth mixture slowly, stirring well to make a smooth cream sauce. Keep hot over a very low flame.

Cook the green pepper in the 2 tablespoons water for 5 minutes. Add the pimiento, mushrooms, and the reserved chicken to the green pepper, cover, and heat through without stirring or boiling. Fold into the cream sauce, stirring as little as possible, then keep warm over a low flame.

Just before serving, transfer the chicken combination to a large casserole and sprinkle the toasted almonds over the top. A moment before serving, pour warmed rum over dish, carefully wield your trusty, long fireplace match, and present the dish, blazing, to your guests. Serve over toast points when the flame dies. (*Serves 8*)

LEFTOVER BONANZA

¼ cup (½ stick) butter
¼ cup all-purpose flour
2 cups chicken broth
Freshly grated horseradish to taste
1 teaspoon granulated sugar
1 teaspoon vinegar
Cold chicken, diced
Rice, noodles, or toast points

Heat the butter in a saucepan, then add the flour and stir until smooth. Add the chicken broth and cook, stirring, until thickened and smooth. Stir in the horseradish, sugar, and vinegar. Taste for seasoning, then add the chicken, heat through, and serve on rice, noodles, or toast points. (*Serves as many as can handle the leftover chicken*)

COCONUT CHICKEN

2 cups heavy cream
1½ cups shredded coconut
2 three-pound fryers, quartered
3 cloves garlic, put through a press
1 small onion, chopped
½ teaspoon cayenne

2 tablespoons peanut butter
1 tablespoon grated lemon rind
6 coriander seeds
1 teaspoon granulated sugar
1 tablespoon soy sauce

Combine the cream and coconut in a large skillet and bring to a boil, then remove from the heat and allow to stand for 30 minutes. Add the chickens to the cooled cream mixture and cook over medium heat for 30 minutes, turning several times to coat with the sauce. Add remaining ingredients and cook about 15 minutes longer, or until the chicken is very tender. (*Serves 8*)

CHICKEN IN A SPINACH RING

1 tablespoon butter
2 tablespoons all-purpose flour
1 cup chicken broth
1 cup evaporated milk
½ teaspoon salt
2 cups diced, cooked chicken
¼ teaspoon grated lemon rind
4 cups cooked, chopped, drained and seasoned spinach

Heat the butter in a saucepan and blend in the flour. Add the broth, milk, and salt and cook just to the boiling point, stirring constantly. Add the chicken and lemon rind. Set aside, but keep warm.

Pack the spinach into a greased 8-inch ring mold, pressing down tightly with the back of a spoon. Place the ring in a pan of hot water and bake in a 350° oven for 20 minutes, then turn out onto a platter. Fill the center with the creamed chicken. (*Serves 6*)

CHICKEN À LA QUEEN VÉRONIQUE

¼ cup (½ stick) butter
3 tablespoons chopped green pepper
6 tablespoons all-purpose flour
1 teaspoon salt
1½ cups hot chicken broth
1½ cups hot milk
3 cups diced, cooked chicken
2½ cups seedless green grapes, fresh or canned
8 individual patty shells

Melt the butter, and when it is bubbly, add the green pepper and cook for 5 minutes. Stir in the flour and salt, then slowly add the hot broth and milk. Cook, stirring until thick and smooth, then stir in the chicken and 2 cups of the grapes and heat thoroughly. Spoon into the patty shells and garnish with the remaining grapes. (*Serves 8*)

17 Curries

How to Curry Flavor with Practically Everybody

There are as many types of curry as there are provinces in India, plus all the other world's regions that have incorporated this luscious amalgam of seeds, spices, and seasonings into their national cuisines.

1. Curry is a wonderful party dish because it takes well to day-before preparation. Reheating a curry actually improves its flavor.

2. Curry does *not* have to blister the palate. Curry powders are sold in mild, medium, and hot intensities, so it is just a matter of individual taste plus a little experimentation on the part of the curry-er.

3. It is traditional to surround the main curry dish with small bowls of various condiments. These little side dishes not only have eye appeal, they add various interesting textures and flavors to the curry itself.

You may use any—or all (although doubtful)—of the following: chopped salted peanuts, chopped hard-cooked egg whites, sieved hard-cooked yolks, chopped watermelon pickles, chopped green olives, crumbled crisp bacon, kumquats, white raisins, dark raisins, crystallized flower petals (violet or rose), shredded Bombay duck (a fish!), pickled walnuts, chopped lemon or lime peel, thinly sliced green onions, crumbled potato chips, orange marmalade, chopped preserved ginger, coconut flakes, and—most important of all —chutney.

4. It is essential to serve rice with curry, and the *only* acceptable drink is cold beer.

5. In Americanized curry recipes clarified butter is used instead of the traditional Indian *ghee.* To clarify, place the prescribed amount of butter in a small saucepan and melt over very low heat. Carefully pour off the clear liquid to use in the recipe and discard the whitish sediment at the bottom of the pan.

The foregoing notes may be tedious, but they're essential to the creation of a noteworthy curry dinner. Let's start cautiously, however, with a:

SIMPLIFIED CHICKEN CURRY

1 four- to five-pound stewing chicken, cooked, boned and cut in large dice
¼ cup clarified butter (see above)
2 to 3 teaspoons good-quality curry powder
½ teaspoon salt
Pinch of cayenne
½ teaspoon ground allspice
½ teaspoon ground mace
½ teaspoon ground ginger
¼ cup all-purpose flour
1½ cups chicken broth
1 cup heavy cream
½ cup apple sauce
Hot, fluffy rice

Keep the chicken hot in the top of a double boiler over simmering water. Heat the clarified butter in a saucepan, then stir in the curry powder, salt, cayenne, and the spices. Blend in the flour until smooth, then add the broth and cream and cook, stirring, until very smooth and thickened. Add the apple sauce and cook another 5 minutes. Taste for seasoning, then blend the chicken into the sauce and serve over hot, fluffy rice. (*Serves 6 to 8*)

BENGAL CURRY

2 three-pound chickens, disjointed
¼ cup clarified butter (see page 187)
1 large onion, chopped fine
¼ cup thinly sliced crystallized ginger
1 teaspoon granulated sugar
Pinch of freshly ground black pepper
Pinch of powdered cloves
1 tablespoon salt
2 tablespoons curry powder
1 teaspoon dried mint or a few leaves of fresh mint
¼ cup all-purpose flour
1 quart whole milk
1 three-and-one-half-ounce can flaked coconut
Juice of 4 limes
2 cups light cream

Cook the chicken in the butter in a Dutch oven until golden brown on all sides, then add the onion and continue to cook until the onion is limp. Season with the ginger, sugar, pepper, cloves, salt, curry powder, and mint. Stir in the flour and blend until smooth. Gradually pour in the milk and blend thoroughly, then cover and cook very slowly for about 1 hour, or until the chicken is quite tender. Stir in the coconut, lime juice, and cream and continue cooking until the mixture is very hot. Serve on a large platter around a mound of cooked rice. (*Serves 8*)

CHICKEN CURRY KORMA

- **2 cloves garlic, halved**
- **1 onion, chopped**
- **1 teaspoon salt**
- **2 teaspoons ginger root, shredded as fine as possible**
- **2 cups plain yogurt**
- **2 pounds chicken breasts, boned, skinned, and diced**
- **½ cup plus 1 tablespoon clarified butter (see page 187)**
- **1 tablespoon ground turmeric**
- **1 teaspoon cumin seeds**
- **½ teaspoon mustard seeds**
- **3 cardamom seeds**
- **3 whole black peppercorns**
- **1 teaspoon good-quality curry powder**
- **⅓ cup hot water, more if necessary**

Pound the garlic, half of the onion, the salt, and ginger in a mortar, or whir in a blender. Mix with the yogurt and chicken and marinate for at least 1 hour, preferably longer.

In a large skillet, lightly brown the remaining onion in the ½ cup butter, then blend in the turmeric. Crush the cumin, mustard and cardamom seeds with the peppercorns. Add, along with the curry powder, to the browned onion and simmer for 1 minute, then add chicken, along with the marinade. Simmer until the sauce is reduced by half, then stir in the 1 tablespoon butter and the hot water. Cover and simmer until chicken is tender (about 15 minutes). (It may be necessary to add a little extra water so the curry does not become too dry.) Serve with or over rice. (*Serves 4*)

ISLAND CURRY

- **¼ cup clarified butter (see page 187)**
- **2 small onions, chopped**
- **1 stalk celery, chopped**
- **1 tart apple, peeled, cored, and diced**
- **¼ cup all-purpose flour**
- **2 teaspoons good-quality curry powder**
- **1½ teaspoons salt**
- **½ teaspoon dry mustard**
- **¼ teaspoon pepper**
- **1 bay leaf**
- **3 cups chicken stock**
- **3 cups large-diced, cooked chicken**
- **1 cup milk**
- **1 cup pineapple chunks**

Heat the butter in a saucepan and sauté the onions, celery, and apple for about 5 minutes, stirring occasionally. Blend in the flour mixed with the curry powder, salt, mustard, and pepper, then add the bay leaf. Gradually add the chicken stock, stirring constantly. Cook over low heat for 15 minutes, stirring occasionally, then remove the bay leaf and add the chicken, milk, and pineapple to the curry mixture. Cook for 3 minutes.

Serve over hot, fluffy rice. (*Serves 6*)

EAST INDIAN CURRY

- **1 four- to five-pound chicken, disjointed**
- **5 cups boiling water to which 1 teaspoon salt has been added**
- **¾ cup finely chopped onion**
- **3 tablespoons peanut oil**
- **1 whole clove**

1 ½ teaspoons good-quality curry powder
1 ½ teaspoons ground turmeric
1 ½ teaspoons ground ginger
1 teaspoon ground cardamom
1 teaspoon dried marjoram
⅓ teaspoon dried thyme
1 small bunch parsley, chopped fine
½ cup finely chopped carrot
¼ cup chopped celery leaves
4 chili peppers, chopped
1 ½ cups coconut milk or 1 ½ cups milk in which shredded coconut has soaked for 2 hours, then been discarded

Cook the chicken in the boiling salted water until tender (about 2 hours). Remove the chicken and set aside, reserving the broth. Sauté the onion in the oil until tender, then add the spices, herbs, and vegetables and blend well. Add the chicken broth and coconut milk, stirring well. Remove chicken from the bones and cut into small pieces, then add to the sauce and simmer for 15 minutes. (*Serves 8*)

ORANGE-COCONUT CURRY

1 teaspoon salt
¼ cup grated orange rind
½ cup grated coconut
2 teaspoons good-quality curry powder
2 cups potato flakes
3 pounds chicken breasts, legs, and thighs
2 eggs, lightly beaten with 1 tablespoon water
Melted butter

Mix the salt, orange rind, coconut, curry powder, and potato flakes. Dip the chicken parts into the beaten egg, then coat heavily with the potato mixture. Place in a well-buttered shallow pan, drizzle melted butter over all, and bake in a 350° oven for 40 to 45 minutes. (*Serves 6 to 8*)

BURMA CURRY

¼ cup peanut oil
1 clove garlic, put through a press
4 red chili peppers, crushed
1 cup minced onion
⅛ teaspoon saffron
3 cups diced, cooked chicken
2 cups chicken broth
¼ cup cold water
1 tablespoon arrowroot

Heat the oil in a heavy skillet and add the garlic, chilies, onion and saffron. Cook over medium heat until the onion is limp, then add the chicken and broth and stir well. Simmer for about 20 minutes. Combine the cold water and arrowroot and stir into the hot curry. Cook, stirring, for 5 minutes, or until the sauce is smooth and thick. (*Serves 4*)

SOUTH INDIAN CHICKEN-CASHEW CURRY

¼ cup peanut oil
1 three-pound fryer, disjointed
1 onion, finely chopped
1 teaspoon ground coriander
½ teaspoon ground turmeric
½ teaspoon cayenne
⅛ teaspoon ground cinnamon
⅛ teaspoon ground cloves

½ teaspoon grated fresh ginger
Pinch of ground cardamom
2 cloves garlic, put through a press
2 teaspoons chopped green pepper
½ cup grated unsweetened coconut
1 teaspoon salt
1 cup plain yogurt
1 cup water
½ cup cashew nuts
1 tablespoon butter
Juice of 1 lime
Mint sprigs for garnish

Heat the oil in a large skillet and brown the chicken parts on both sides. Remove and set aside. Fry the onion in the remaining oil until golden, then add the spices and garlic and cook for 3 minutes. Stir in the green pepper, coconut, salt, yogurt, and water, then add the chicken, cover, and simmer until the chicken is tender (about 20 minutes).

Meanwhile, sauté the cashew nuts in butter. When the chicken is done, stir in the nuts and lime juice. Garnish with mint sprigs and serve with rice. (*Serves 6 to 8*)

CHICKEN-LOBSTER CURRY

- 2½ cups hot milk
- 3 cups shredded coconut
- ½ cup clarified butter (see page 187)
- 2 cloves garlic, halved
- 1 cup chopped onion
- ¼ teaspoon ground ginger
- 2 teaspoons good-quality curry powder
- 2 cups chicken broth
- ½ cup all-purpose flour
- 1 teaspoon salt
- 1 tablespoon lemon juice
- 1 cup half-and-half
- 3 cups diced, cooked chicken
- 4 lobster tails
- 6 to 8 cups hot, cooked rice

Pour the hot milk over the coconut and let stand for 30 minutes. Heat ¼ cup of the clarified butter in a skillet, add the garlic and onion, and cook until the onion is limp. Add the ginger, curry powder, broth, and coconut-milk mixture. Cover and simmer for 30 minutes, stirring occasionally, then remove from the heat and strain, discarding the coconut, garlic, and onion.

Heat the remaining ¼ cup butter in a large saucepan. Stir in the flour and strained liquid, then cook and stir until smooth and slightly thickened. Stir in the salt, lemon juice, half-and-half, and cooked chicken and cook until the chicken is heated through.

Meanwhile, cut the lobster tails into halves lengthwise and cook in boiling salted water for about 6 minutes, or until just tender. Remove the shells and keep the meat warm. Place the cooked rice in a large serving dish and pour the hot chicken mixture over it. Arrange the lobster meat on top and serve. (*Serves 6 to 8*)

CURRIED CHICKEN MAHARANI

- ¼ cup clarified butter (see page 187)
- 1 bunch green onions, chopped fine
- 2 green pippin apples, peeled, cored, and chopped
- ½ banana, mashed
- 1 tablespoon arrowroot
- 1 cup chicken broth
- 1 cup half-and-half
- Salt and freshly ground pepper to taste
- ¼ teaspoon ground ginger
- 1 level tablespoon good-quality curry powder
- 3 cups diced, cooked chicken

Heat the butter in a large skillet and cook the onions over low heat until limp. Add the apples and banana and mash all together, then add the arrowroot and blend well. Add the broth slowly, stirring constantly to keep smooth. Blend in the half-and-half and continue stirring until the mixture thickens, then add the salt, pepper, ginger, and curry powder, blending well. Transfer the mixture to the top of a double boiler and place over boiling water. Add the chicken and cook until the chicken is heated through. (*Serves 6*)

CURRIED CHICKEN RAJ

- 2 two-and-one-half-pound fryers, quartered
- 1 teaspoon monosodium glutamate
- 1 eight-ounce can jellied cranberry sauce
- 1 cup red currant jelly
- ¼ cup garlic wine vinegar
- 3 tablespoons peanut oil
- 3 teaspoons Worcestershire sauce
- Salt and freshly ground pepper to taste
- 3 teaspoons good-quality curry powder
- 4 drops Tabasco

Sprinkle the chicken quarters with the monosodium glutamate and set aside. In a saucepan, melt the cranberry and currant jellies, then add the remaining ingredients and stir over low heat until the mixture is thoroughly blended. Put the chicken into a shallow baking pan, spoon the sauce over, and bake in a 350° oven for about 50 minutes, or until the chicken is very tender, being sure to baste frequently while the chicken is baking. (*Serves 8*)

POT-ROASTED CURRIED CHICKEN

1 four- to five-pound young roasting chicken
Salt and freshly ground pepper to taste
1 teaspoon grated fresh ginger
⅓ cup butter
2½ cups chicken broth
1 cup minced onion
1 cup peeled, cored, and chopped pippin apples
1 heaping tablespoon curry powder
2 tablespoons all-purpose flour
1 cup light cream
1 tablespoon lemon juice
2 cups hot, cooked rice

Truss the chicken to fit a Dutch oven. Combine the salt, pepper, and ginger and rub it into the chicken, then melt half the butter in the Dutch oven and brown the chicken on all sides. Add the chicken broth, bring to a low boil, and simmer, covered, for 20 to 25 minutes.

In a skillet, melt the remaining butter and cook the onion and apple, stirring constantly, for 10 minutes. Add the curry powder and blend well. Add the mixture to the chicken, stirring it around the fowl so the seasonings are well blended. Cover and simmer for 45 minutes, turning chicken several times during the cooking period. When the chicken is tender, remove it to a hot platter and keep hot while you finish the sauce.

Mix together the flour and cream, adding the cream a little at a time so the mixture stays smooth. Slowly add it to the sauce in the Dutch oven, stirring constantly. Cook a few minutes, until the sauce thickens, then pour the lemon juice, drop by drop, into the sauce, stirring all the while and continue to stir for another 5 minutes while it cooks gently.

Put the rice into a serving dish, top with the chicken, and pour the sauce over all. (*Serves 6*)

COLD CURRIED CHICKEN RANCHIPUR

This is eminently successful as the pièce de résistance on a summer buffet table, and is easily cooked and assembled a day or two before serving.

½ cup clarified butter (see page 187)
2 four- to five-pound roasting chickens, disjointed
3 tablespoons brandy
2 large onions, quartered and sliced
1 tablespoon salt
1 teaspoon freshly ground pepper
½ cup water
2 tablespoons good-quality curry powder
Sliced green and black olives
Pimiento cut in strips or fancy shapes
2 cups heavy cream
Crisp endive leaves, whole olives, and cherry tomatoes for garnish

Heat all but 2 tablespoons of the butter in a large skillet and brown the chicken pieces lightly on all sides. Transfer to a Dutch oven, in which the remaining butter has been heated. Gently heat the brandy, pour over the chicken, and blaze (don't forget to use a long fireplace match!). When the flame dies, cover the chicken with the onion slices and sprinkle with the salt and pepper. Pour ½ cup water into the skillet in which the chicken was browned and scrape up all the brown goodness. Pour this over the chicken, cover, and simmer gently for about 1 hour, or until the meat is just about ready to fall off the bones. Sprinkle the curry powder over the chicken and baste well, then simmer for another 3 minutes. Remove from the fire and allow to cool (the chicken *must* cool in its own liquid). When it is cool enough to handle, remove the chicken from Dutch oven, skin it, bone it, and remove all gristle. Cut the breasts in half lengthwise.

In a 6 x 10 x 2-inch baking dish, arrange a design of sliced olives and pimiento strips or fancy shapes. Carefully lay the breast pieces over the design and press down, then arrange the rest of the chicken over the breasts. Put the Dutch oven back on a low flame, add the cream, and heat just to boiling. Pour this sauce through a sieve into a large bowl, pressing down on the onion slices to remove all the sauce. Discard the onion. Taste the sauce for seasoning, then pour very carefully over the chicken in the dish, making sure your olive-pimiento design is not disarranged. Cover the dish and refrigerate until just before serving; it should be perfectly jelled.

To unmold, run a knife blade around the edges of the curry, dip mold in hot water for a moment, and invert onto a large, chilled platter. Garnish with crisp leaves of endive, whole olives, and cherry tomatoes. (*Serves 8 to 10*)

18 Mousses

How to Cook a Mousse, and Other Cold Birds

It's summer. The weather is warm-to-torrid. The patio, terrace, garden, balcony, and/or fire escape are too tropical to be borne. You're up to *here* with the blast furnace-cum-barbecue. And guests are expected! Just open up the refrigerator—and keep your cool!

FAIRLY BASIC CHICKEN MOUSSE

3 tablespoons butter
3 tablespoons all-purpose flour
2 cups chicken stock, strained
2 cups ground, cooked chicken
1 teaspoon grated onion
2 envelopes unflavored gelatin
1 tablespoon sherry
2 cups heavy cream, whipped
Salt and freshly ground pepper to taste
Watercress, cherry tomatoes, and ripe olives for garnish

Melt the butter over low heat and stir in the flour. Gradually add 1 cup of the stock and cook, stirring constantly, until smooth and thick. Add the ground chicken and grated onion and set aside.

Soften the gelatin in another ½ cup of the stock, then bring the remaining ½ cup stock to a boil, add the softened gelatin, and stir until dissolved. Add the sherry and set aside to cool. When the ingredients have completely cooled, combine the chicken, sauce, and gelatin mixture. Fold in the whipped cream and season to taste. Pour the mixture into an oiled 2-quart mold and chill for at least 2 hours, or until firm.

Unmold onto a chilled platter and garnish with watercress, cherry tomatoes, and ripe olives. Serve with an herb-flavored mayonnaise. (*Serves 8*)

MANYA'S MOUSSE

1 envelope unflavored gelatin
½ cup sherry
1 cup chicken stock, strained
1½ tablespoons minced chives
1 cup chopped, cooked chicken
½ cup chopped, cooked ham
½ cup chopped, cooked tongue
½ cup chopped, cooked mushrooms
½ cup chopped walnuts
Salt and freshly ground pepper to taste
2 cups heavy cream, whipped

Soften the gelatin in the sherry. Heat the stock to boiling, then remove from the heat and stir in the gelatin until it dissolves. Cool the mixture and pour a little into an oiled mold. Refrigerate. When it sets, sprinkle with the minced chives. Add the remainder of the gelatin and allow to set again.

Combine the chicken, ham, tongue, mushrooms, nuts, salt, and pepper. Fold in the whipped cream and fill the remainder of the mold with the mixture. Chill for at least 2 hours or overnight.

Unmold onto a chilled platter and serve with mayonnaise thinned with a little lemon juice and mixed with minced chives. (*Serves 6 to 8*)

ICED COLD CHICKEN

- **2 two-and-one-half-pound fryers, disjointed, livers reserved**
- **½ cup (1 stick) butter**
- **Salt**
- **Lemon juice**
- **1 clove garlic, peeled**
- **1 cup mayonnaise**
- **1 teaspoon Dijon mustard**
- **¾ cup heavy cream, whipped**
- **Chopped chives**
- **Capers**
- **Tomato aspic and watercress for garnish**

Sauté the chickens in the butter until tender, then drain on paper toweling and allow to cool. Remove the skin and discard.

Cook the chicken livers in salted water, and when done, chop coarsely. Squeeze a little lemon juice over them. Drop the clove of garlic into a blender container, along with the livers. Add just enough mayonnaise so the blender operates without straining and whir until the mixture becomes a smooth paste. Combine this paste with the remaining mayonnaise, the mustard, and lemon juice to taste. Carefully fold in the whipped cream, then, just as though you were frosting a cake, generously spread the mixture on top of each chicken piece. Chill well.

To serve, place the chicken pieces on a chilled platter and sprinkle liberally with chopped chives and capers. Surround with tomato aspic cut in star shapes and sprigs of watercress. (*Serves 8*)

MICKEY'S MOUSSE

2 envelopes unflavored gelatin
2 cups chicken broth
⅓ cup chopped green onions
1 teaspoon salt
1 teaspoon grated lemon rind
1 cup dry white wine
1 teaspoon Worcestershire sauce
1 cup heavy cream, whipped
1 cup mayonnaise
3 tablespoons diced, canned peeled green chilies
2 cups chopped, cooked chicken
1 cup chopped, cooked ham
3 tablespoons minced fresh parsley
Watercress and spiced peach and pear halves for garnish

Soften the gelatin in ½ cup of the broth. Heat the remaining broth to the boiling point, add the softened gelatin, and stir until it has dissolved. Add the green onions, salt, and grated lemon rind, then blend in the wine and Worcestershire sauce. Chill until the mixture thickens, then fold in the whipped cream, mayonnaise, and diced chilies. Add the chicken, ham, and parsley and blend gently but thoroughly. Pour into an oiled 2½-quart mold and refrigerate until firm.

Unmold on a chilled platter and surround with watercress. Garnish with spiced peach and pear halves. (*Serves 6 to 8*)

LEAN LADY'S MOUSSE

Just 170 calories per serving!

- **2 envelopes unflavored gelatin**
- **1 cup cold water**
- **1 cup boiling water**
- **2 cups diced, cooked chicken**
- **1 cup diced, cooked ham**
- **½ cup mashed avocado**
- **1 cup chopped celery**
- **1 cup chopped water chestnuts**
- **1½ tablespoons grated onion**
- **1 teaspoon salt**
- **2 teaspoons dry mustard**
- **¼ teaspoon freshly ground pepper**
- **2 teaspoons lemon juice**
- **½ cup powdered nonfat dry milk**

Soften the gelatin in ½ cup of the cold water, then add the boiling water and stir until the gelatin dissolves. Add the chicken, ham, avocado, celery, water chestnuts, onion, salt, mustard, and pepper and chill until the mixture thickens slightly.

Meanwhile, combine the remaining ½ cup cold water, the lemon juice and powdered milk in a small bowl. Whip until stiff (about 6 minutes), then fold into the gelatin mixture. Pour into an oiled 1½-quart mold and chill overnight before unmolding. (*Serves 8*)

SOUR CREAM MOUSSE

2 envelopes unflavored gelatin
½ cup cold water
2 cups very strong chicken broth
3 tablespoons lemon juice
1 teaspoon dry mustard
2½ teaspoons good-quality curry powder
1 teaspoon onion salt
2 cups sour cream
3 cups diced, cooked chicken
1 cup chopped celery
¼ cup chopped green pepper
¼ cup diced, roasted almonds
Watercress, stuffed green olives, and cherry tomatoes for garnish

In a large bowl, sprinkle the gelatin over the cold water. When softened, pour the boiling chicken broth over the gelatin and stir until dissolved. Add the lemon juice, mustard, curry powder, and onion salt and allow to cool for 5 minutes. Stir in the sour cream, mixing well, then refrigerate until the mixture begins to thicken. Fold in the chicken, celery, green pepper, and almonds, then turn the mixture into an oiled 1½-quart mold. Refrigerate, covered, until the mousse is firm (at least 2 hours).

To serve, turn out onto a chilled platter and garnish with watercress sprigs, stuffed green olives, and cherry tomatoes. (*Serves 8*)

SIMPLE JELLIED CHICKEN LOAF

- 1 envelope unflavored gelatin
- ¼ cup cold water
- 2 cups hot chicken broth
- ¼ cup mayonnaise
- 2 teaspoons soy sauce
- 2½ cups diced, cooked chicken
- ½ cup diced celery
- 2 tablespoons finely chopped walnuts

Soften the gelatin in the cold water. Stir into the broth and heat, stirring constantly, just until the gelatin dissolves. Stir in the mayonnaise and soy sauce, then pour into a 6-cup mold. Chill until as thick as unbeaten egg white, then stir in the remaining ingredients. Chill several hours, until very firm. Unmold and serve with crusty French bread. (*Serves 6*)

JELLIED CHICKEN PIE

- 2 chicken breasts, skinned, boned, and halved
- 10 mushrooms, sliced
- 2 tablespoons chopped onion
- 1 tablespoon chopped fresh parsley
- ½ teaspoon Worcestershire sauce
- Salt and freshly ground pepper to taste
- ½ cup sherry
- 4 cups extra-strong chicken broth
- Rich pastry for a 1-crust pie
- 4 slices cooked ham, cut in strips
- 2 hard-cooked eggs, sliced
- Chopped fresh parsley for garnish

Place the chicken-breast pieces in the bottom of a casserole and cover with the mushrooms, onion, parsley, Worcestershire sauce, salt, pepper, sherry, and 3 cups of the chicken broth (setting aside the remaining broth to use as a glaze). Top with the pastry, slashed in a "daisy" design, and bake in a 350° oven for 50 to 60 minutes, then cool and chill in the refrigerator until the jelly is set. If pastry begins to brown too much, cover with a round of buttered paper.

When the jelly is set, carefully lift off the top crust and add the ham and eggs to the filling. Replace the crust and cover it with a glaze of almost-set chicken broth. Garnish the top with chopped parsley and serve. (*Serves 8*)

Note: If the broth is extra-strong, the whole thing will jell like a dream! If you use a thin, canned broth, gelatin may be needed.

CHICKEN CITRON

1 three-and-one-half-pound fryer
1 onion, stuck with 4 cloves
2 cloves garlic
1 carrot
4 sprigs fresh parsley
2 teaspoons salt
5 peppercorns
Peel of 1 lemon, slivered
Juice of ½ lemon
¼ cup sherry
1 cup half-and-half
2 egg yolks
⅓ cup halved almonds

Put the chicken in a kettle, almost cover with water, add the onion, garlic, carrot, parsley, salt, peppercorns, and half the lemon peel. Simmer until the chicken is tender (about

1½ hours), then remove from the heat and allow the chicken to cool in the broth. When cool, remove the skin and bones and cut the meat into good-sized pieces. Set aside.

Strain the stock and measure 1½ cups of it into a saucepan. Bring to a boil, then add the remaining lemon peel, slivered, the lemon juice, and sherry. Taste for seasoning and cook for 5 minutes. Stir in the half-and-half mixed with the egg yolks and cook over low heat, stirring constantly, for 2 minutes more, or until the sauce thickens slightly. Combine it with the cooked chicken, turn the mixture into a glass bowl, and chill thoroughly. Sprinkle with the almonds and serve very cold. (*Serves 8*)

CHILLED CHICKEN MAISON

1 envelope unflavored gelatin
¼ cup cold water
1 cup strong, hot chicken broth
3 tablespoons butter
3 tablespoons all-purpose flour
¼ teaspoon salt
2 tablespoons heavy cream
¼ cup frozen orange juice concentrate
3 cooked chicken breasts, skinned, boned, and halved

Soften the gelatin in the cold water and add to the hot chicken broth. Melt the butter in a saucepan and stir in the flour. Add the broth and salt and bring to a boil, stirring. Remove from the heat. Gradually add the cream and orange juice, stirring constantly. Place the pan in a large bowl of ice cubes and stir until cold but not set.

Arrange the chicken breasts on a serving platter and cover with the sauce. Chill and serve very cold. (*Serves 6*)

PRESSED CHICKEN CALIFORNIA

1 envelope unflavored gelatin
¼ cup cold water
2 cups boiling chicken broth
Salt and freshly ground pepper to taste
Spice Islands Beau Monde seasoning (optional)
4 hard-cooked eggs
2 cups chopped, cooked chicken
1 cup diced celery
¼ cup chopped fresh parsley
Fresh parsley or watercress for garnish

Soften the gelatin in the cold water. Add to the boiling chicken broth and stir until the gelatin dissolves. Season with salt, pepper, and Spice Islands Beau Monde seasoning, if desired, to taste, then chill the mixture until thick but not set. Meanwhile, chop the egg whites and yolks separately.

Layer the ingredients in an oiled loaf pan (8½ x 4½ x ½ inches), starting with 1 cup of the chicken. Add a layer of egg whites, then celery and parsley mixed, then a layer of egg yolks, then top with the remaining chicken. Carefully pour the broth over all, making sure the layers are not disturbed. Cover and chill until firm.

Unmold on a serving platter, surround with fresh parsley or watercress, and serve with mayonnaise thinned with a little lemon juice and sparked with curry powder. (*Serves 6*)

JELLIED CHICKEN GALA

- 2 envelopes unflavored gelatin
- 4 cups strong chicken broth
- Salt and freshly ground pepper to taste
- Pinch of cayenne
- 1 large pimiento, cut into strips
- 4 cooked chicken breasts, skinned, boned, and sliced
- 1½ cups each cooked peas, baby lima beans, green beans, and sliced carrots
- Cherry tomatoes, sweet gherkins, and stuffed olives for garnish

Soften the gelatin in 1 cup cold chicken broth. Heat the remaining 3 cups and add the gelatin mixture, stirring until dissolved. Season to taste with salt, pepper, and cayenne, then chill until syrupy.

Arrange the pimiento strips on the bottom of an oiled 2-quart mold and place the chicken slices on top. Arrange the cooked vegetables over the chicken. Pour the syrupy gelatin over all, lifting the vegetables and chicken carefully so the gelatin can penetrate each layer. Chill thoroughly.

Unmold on a chilled platter and surround with cherry tomatoes, sweet gherkins, and stuffed olives. (*Serves 8*)

COLD CHICKEN MICHOACÁN

- ½ cup good-quality olive oil
- 2 two-pound chickens, halved
- 4 cloves garlic
- Salt and freshly ground pepper to taste
- 4 whole cloves
- 4 allspice berries
- ½ teaspoon each dried rosemary, thyme, and sweet basil

1⅓ cups wine vinegar
2⅔ cups white wine
4 tablespoons chopped fresh parsley

Heat the oil in a skillet and brown the chicken halves and 1 clove of the garlic. Remove the chicken to a deep casserole. Season well with salt and pepper, sprinkle with all the spices and herbs except the parsley, add the remaining garlic, and pour the vinegar over all. Set aside.

Heat the wine with the oil and drippings in the skillet in which the chickens were browned, scraping up all the good crunchy bits. When the mixture just comes to a boil, pour over the chickens in the casserole. Cover and bake in a 350° oven for 1½ hours, or until the chicken is tender, then transfer the fowl to 4 deep plates and strain the liquid over. Sprinkle with parsley and chill thoroughly.

Before serving, scrape off all visible fat. The chicken halves may be served in the plates in which they were chilled. (*Serves 4*)

CHICKEN EGG RING

1 envelope unflavored gelatin
¼ cup cold water
1 cup chicken stock
2½ cups ground, cooked chicken
½ cup chopped celery
¼ cup chopped sweet pickles
½ cup French dressing
¼ teaspoon salt
Freshly ground pepper
3 hard-cooked eggs, sliced
Greens of your choice for garnish

Soften the gelatin in the cold water for 5 minutes. Dissolve over hot water, then stir into the chicken stock and chill until slightly thickened. Add all the other ingredients except the eggs and greens.

Arrange the egg slices in a lightly oiled 1-quart ring mold. Pour in a little of the chicken mixture and chill to keep the egg slices in place. Fill mold with the remaining chicken mixture and chill until firm.

Unmold on a serving platter and fill with greens of your choice. Serve with a side dish of parsleyed mayonnaise. (*Serves 4 to 6*)

CHICKEN IN ASPIC

2 envelopes unflavored gelatin
¼ cup cold water
2 cups chicken stock
1 eight-ounce can pitted cherries, drained, but 1 tablespoon juice reserved
Salt and freshly ground pepper to taste
8 to 10 ounces cooked chicken, sliced

Dissolve the gelatin in the cold water. Heat the stock and add the dissolved gelatin, stirring. Add the reserved cherry juice, salt, and pepper, stir well, and remove from the heat. Refrigerate the aspic in a loaf pan until it begins to thicken, then add the chicken and cherries.

Unmold on a serving platter and surround with small bunches of grapes, watercress, or whatever strikes your fancy. A slightly sweetened mayonnaise is an excellent dressing for this. (*Serves 4 to 6*)

19 Rotisserie and Grill

Cooking Inside/Outside

I'm the only person allowed to do any spitting around my house . . . mainly because the sound of a lazily revolving rotisserie is music to my ears and balm to my soul. The end result is invariably superb—a crisp-skinned bird erupting aromatic juices that are almost maddeningly delicious!

A few ground rules:

1. I recommend that you do *not* wash a chicken to be spitted. Instead, rub it thoroughly with a cut lemon. Anoint the body cavity with a mixture of lemon juice and butter or margarine, plus one of the herbs indicated in the marinade and/or basting sauce.

2. To prepare the chicken for its culinary carousel, fold the wings over the back, hooking the wing tips behind the shoulder joints, and tie well. Skewer the neck skin in place. Tie the legs to the tail piece and draw close to the body. Spit the bird lengthwise, secure the spit prongs, and make sure the bird or birds are centered and well balanced. A meat thermometer in the thickest part of the thigh should register 170° when the chicken is done.

3. When using a charcoal grill, adjust it to 6 or 8 inches above the firebed (which must consist of a layer of good, hot coals neatly blanketed with gray ash—a point reached approximately 45 minutes after starting the fire). Brush the chickens—either halved, quartered, or disjointed—generously with oil or margarine, and place on the grill, skin side up. Turn the chicken several times during the cooking period, and baste it frequently with sauce. About 45 to 50 minutes of cooking time should be enough to bring the bird to tenderness, but there is no set rule. Each bird differs; each bed of coals throws off a different degree of heat. But in any case, *never overcook*! And since white meat cooks faster than dark, watch it! The chicken is done when the leg twists easily in the thigh joint, or when the tip of a sharp knife thrust into a joint reveals no pink flesh.

Having dispensed with the ground rules, we now progress to the basting sauces and marinades. There are several exceptionally good bottled barbecue sauces on the market. Don't hesitate to try them. I am personally inclined to Chris & Pitt's because of its pungent and robust flavor. And while actually not a sauce, Wright's Bar-B-Q Smoke is deliciously unique. Simply slather the chicken with this liquid smoke, allow it to dry, sprinkle with salt and pepper and consign it to either spit or grill. The Wright people have literally captured the essence of hickory in this modestly priced bottle. Liquid smoke adds the outdoor taste of summer even to a midwinter indoor barbecue. Here, first, are basting sauce recipes for either spit or grill. Each recipe should bathe 2 two-and-one-half- to three-pound birds.

JENNY'S BASTER

½ cup (1 stick) butter
Juice of ½ large lemon
¼ cup honey
3 large cloves garlic, put through a press

Combine all the ingredients in a saucepan, heat, and baste the chicken copiously with the mixture.

HERBAL BASTING SAUCE

1 cup (2 sticks) softened butter
2 tablespoons dried rosemary or tarragon, crumbled
Salt and freshly ground pepper to taste

Combine all the ingredients. Carefully separate the skin from the breasts, thighs, and drumsticks of your chickens and coat the exposed flesh with the herbed and seasoned butter. Secure the loosened skin with small metal skewers.

Note: If you are fortunate enough to boast your own herb garden, snip several twigs of whichever herb you elect to use, tie them together at one end, and use them to swab the bird with the heated sauce during the cooking process.

JAMAICAN BASTER

½ cup (1 stick) melted butter
2 tablespoons lime juice
2 teaspoons salt
1 teaspoon ground allspice
1 teaspoon garlic powder
1 teaspoon onion powder
¼ teaspoon cayenne

Blend all the ingredients in a saucepan and heat before brushing on the birds.

PIQUANT BASTER

Salad oil
½ cup mayonnaise
½ cup catsup
2 tablespoons vinegar

1 tablespoon Worcestershire sauce
1 tablespoon finely minced onion
1 tablespoon prepared horseradish
Salt, cayenne, and freshly ground pepper to taste

Brush the chickens with salad oil, then blend the remaining ingredients and use as a basting sauce.

LEMON BASTING SAUCE

1 large clove garlic, put through a press
¼ cup salad oil
½ teaspoon salt
½ teaspoon freshly ground pepper
½ cup lemon juice
2 tablespoons grated onion
½ teaspoon dried thyme, crumbled

Combine all the ingredients and chill for 24 hours before using to baste the chickens.

RITZ BASTING SAUCE

½ cup (1 stick) melted butter
⅓ cup sherry or Sauterne
1 teaspoon dried oregano, crumbled
1 teaspoon minced fresh parsley
Salt and freshly ground pepper to taste

Combine the ingredients in a saucepan and heat before brushing on the chickens.

PICKLED BASTER

- 1 six-ounce can tomato paste
- 1 cup finely chopped dill pickle
- ¼ cup finely chopped onion
- 2 tablespoons vinegar
- 1 tablespoon honey
- 2 tablespoons soy sauce
- ¼ teaspoon dry mustard
- 1⅓ cups water

Combine the ingredients in a saucepan and bring to a boil. Let simmer for at least 15 minutes before using.

LOUISIANA BASTER

- 1 teaspoon dry mustard
- 1 teaspoon salt
- ¼ teaspoon garlic powder
- ¼ cup vinegar
- ½ cup salad oil
- ½ teaspoon Tabasco
- 1 tablespoon unsulphured molasses

Combine all the ingredients in a saucepan and heat before using.

The following recipes are for marinades that can also be used as basting sauces. Except where otherwise indicated, simply blend the ingredients well (shaking them in a jar is a simple method), and pour them over chicken halves, quarters, or pieces in a shallow container. Cover and refrigerate overnight, turning the chicken in its fragrant bath at least twice.

PURPLE PLUM MARINADE

1 one-pound can purple plums (there is an excellent dietetic brand on the market)
1 large onion, sliced
1 large clove garlic, put through a press
2 tablespoons wine vinegar
1 teaspoon salt
1 tablespoon pickling spices, tied in a piece of cheesecloth
¼ cup salad oil

Drain and pit the plums, reserving the syrup. Separate the onion slices into rings and add to the plums. Combine the plum syrup, garlic, vinegar, salt, and pickling spices in a saucepan, heat just to boiling, and pour over the plums and onion. Cover and marinate overnight in refrigerator. The next day, remove the plums and onion from the marinade, place in a small serving dish, and refrigerate until dinner time, when they will be passed as a relish. Discard the spice bag and add the oil to the marinade. Pour over the chicken parts, cover, and refrigerate for at least 4 hours. Cook the chicken as desired, using the marinade as a basting sauce.

PINEAPPLE-LEMON MARINADE

1 six-ounce can frozen pineapple-lemon punch concentrate
½ cup water
1 small clove garlic, put through a press
½ cup salad oil
1 teaspoon powdered ginger
2 tablespoons soy sauce

Combine all the ingredients in a saucepan and bring to a boil. Simmer for 5 minutes, then pour over the chicken, cover, and refrigerate for at least 24 hours.

WEST INDIES MARINADE

½ cup lime juice
½ cup salad oil
½ teaspoon garlic powder
Generous pinch of freshly grated nutmeg
Pinch of ground cardamom
Salt and freshly ground pepper to taste
¼ teaspoon dried chervil

Combine all the ingredients and proceed as directed on page 217.

ORIENTAL MARINADE

1 cup soy sauce
1 cup Japanese rice wine (sake)
1 teaspoon granulated sugar
1 teaspoon grated or shredded fresh ginger
¼ cup salad oil
Dash of sesame oil

Combine all the ingredients and proceed as directed on page 217.

WINE MARINADE

- ¼ cup salad oil
- ½ cup dry white wine
- 1 clove garlic, put through a press
- 1 onion, grated
- ½ teaspoon each salt, freshly ground pepper, and celery salt
- ¼ teaspoon each dried thyme, marjoram, and rosemary

Combine all the ingredients and proceed as directed on page 217.

GREAT WESTERN MARINADE

- ½ cup catsup
- ½ cup minced onion
- ½ cup water
- ⅓ cup salad oil
- ¼ cup lemon juice
- 2 tablespoons brown sugar
- 2 tablespoons Worcestershire sauce
- 1½ teaspoons salt
- 1 teaspoon prepared mustard
- Freshly ground pepper to taste

Combine all the ingredients and proceed as directed on page 217.

WAIKIKI MARINADE

- ⅔ cup soy sauce
- ½ teaspoon sesame oil
- ⅓ cup salad oil
- 3 tablespoons granulated sugar
- ⅓ cup sherry

Combine all the ingredients and proceed as directed on page 217.

20 Foreign Intrigue

Chicken is an original member of the international set—a true citizen of the world. Virtually every nation celebrates the glorious bird in various delectable ways, and waiving passport and visas, I am pleased to offer a generous smattering of these ethnic edibles.

ALGERIAN CHICKEN

1 three-and-one-half-pound chicken, disjointed
Salt and freshly ground pepper to taste
¼ cup (½ stick) butter
⅔ cup dry white wine, more if necessary
6 green onions, chopped
2 large tomatoes, peeled, seeded, and chopped
2 cloves garlic, put through a press
1 medium eggplant, peeled and chopped
⅓ teaspoon dried thyme

Season the chicken parts with salt and pepper and brown lightly in the butter in a large skillet. Remove the chicken from the skillet and add the wine, stirring with a wooden spoon to get up all the good brown bits. Add the onions, tomatoes, garlic, and eggplant and cook for 2 minutes, stirring constantly. Return the chicken to the pan, sprinkle with the thyme, cover, and simmer for 30 to 40 minutes, or until bird is fork tender. (If the liquid evaporates too rapidly, add a little more wine.) (*Serves 4 to 6*)

AUSTRIAN CHICKEN WITH SAUERKRAUT

1½ pounds sauerkraut
1 three-pound chicken, disjointed
Salt and freshly ground pepper to taste
Scant ½ cup bacon drippings
½ cup chopped onion
¼ teaspoon garlic powder
1 tablespoon finely chopped chili peppers
½ cup chicken broth

Soak the sauerkraut in cold water for 15 minutes, then rinse and squeeze dry. Season the chicken parts with salt and pepper and brown them on both sides in half the bacon drippings. Remove the chicken from the pan and add the remaining drippings. When hot, add the onion and cook until transparent. Sprinkle with the garlic powder, add the sauerkraut, and stir. Add the chili peppers and cook, uncovered, for 10 minutes, then return the chicken to the pan, laying the pieces on top of the sauerkraut. Pour the broth over all.

Bring the liquid to a quick boil, then reduce the heat and cook at a simmer, uncovered, for 30 to 40 minutes, or until the chicken is quite tender. (*Serves 4 to 6*)

BELGIAN-STYLE CHICKEN

- 1 three-and-one-half-pound chicken, disjointed
- 2 cups water
- 1½ bay leaves
- 1 stalk celery
- 1 medium-sized onion stuck with 2 whole cloves
- Salt and freshly ground pepper to taste
- ⅛ teaspoon dried thyme
- 2 tablespoons all-purpose flour
- 2 egg yolks
- 2 tablespoons lemon juice
- 1 teaspoon granulated sugar
- Lemon slices for garnish

Put the cut-up chicken in a Dutch oven or other pot with a very tight-fitting lid. Add the water, bay leaves, celery, onion, salt, pepper, and thyme. Cover and bring to a boil, then reduce the heat and simmer for 1 hour.

Remove the chicken from the broth and set aside. Strain the broth, then measure 1½ cups of it and return to the pot. Stir another ¼ cup broth into the flour to make a smooth paste, then add the mixture to the broth in the pot, stirring constantly. Bring to a boil.

Meanwhile, beat the egg yolks, lemon juice, and sugar together. Gradually add to the broth, stirring constantly until thickened. Return the chicken to the pot and heat thoroughly but do not boil. Garnish with lemon slices and serve. (*Serves 4*)

BURMESE CHICKEN AND NOODLES

- 1 three-and-one-half-pound fryer, disjointed
- 1 teaspoon saffron
- 1 quart boiling water
- 1 tablespoon salt

2½ cups chopped onion
3 cloves garlic, put through a press
2 teaspoons minced fresh ginger
½ teaspoon dried chili pepper
¼ cup vegetable oil
2 tablespoons all-purpose flour
1½ cups evaporated milk, undiluted
1 pound fine egg noodles, cooked and drained
Chopped, hard-cooked egg, diced cucumbers, and sliced green onions for garnish

Rub the chicken parts with the saffron, then place in the boiling water with the salt and cook over low heat for about 45 minutes, or until tender. Remove the chicken to a platter and continue cooking the stock, uncovered, until it is reduced to 2 cups. Remove the chicken meat from the bone and cut into large dice.

With a mortar and pestle, or in a blender, reduce the onion, garlic, ginger, and chili pepper to a paste. Toss with the chicken, then heat the oil in a deepish skillet and brown the chicken mixture in it. Add the stock and cook over medium heat for 20 minutes. Mix the flour with the milk and stir into the pan. Cook over low heat, stirring constantly, until thickened, then cook 5 minutes longer. Taste for seasoning. Pour over the noodles and garnish with chopped hard-cooked egg, diced cucumbers, and sliced green onions. (*Serves 4 to 6*)

CHILEAN COLD PICKLED CHICKEN

1 three-and-one-half-pound chicken, disjointed
1/3 cup vegetable oil
1 cup dry white wine
1 cup white vinegar
1 cup hot water
2 onions, cut in thin wedges
3 carrots, peeled and sliced thin
1 leek, including a small part of the green top, cleaned and cut into thin rounds
1 tablespoon salt
Bouquet garni (1 celery top, 2 sprigs fresh parsley, 2 bay leaves, 2 whole cloves, and 1/4 teaspoon dried thyme tied in a cheesecloth square)
1 lemon, cut in thin wedges

Brown the chicken parts in very hot oil. Add the wine, vinegar, water, onions, carrots, leek, salt, and bouquet garni. Bring to a quick, rolling boil, then reduce the heat, cover, and simmer for 30 minutes or more, until the chicken is fork tender. Remove the bouquet garni and discard.

Arrange the chicken in a single layer in a deep serving dish and pour the liquid and vegetables over it. Cool. Decorate with lemon wedges, then refrigerate, covered, until the liquid has jelled—at least 6 hours. (*Serves 4 to 6*)

CHINESE CHICKEN AND SHRIMP IMPERIAL

2 tablespoons sesame oil
1 cup diced, raw chicken
1 1/2 tablespoons cornstarch
1 pound small shrimp, shelled and deveined
2 teaspoons finely chopped fresh ginger
2 tablespoons soy sauce

1 teaspoon salt
3 tablespoons sherry
½ teaspoon granulated sugar

Heat the sesame oil in a deep frying pan or Chinese wok and add the chicken, which has been dredged in the cornstarch. Stir-fry over high heat for only 5 or 6 seconds, then add the shrimp and stir-fry for 2 to 3 minutes. Add the remaining ingredients, stirring constantly, and bring just to a boil. Serve at once with any appropriate Chinese accompaniment—fried or boiled rice or fried noodles. (*Serves 4*)

EGYPTIAN CHICKEN KEBABS

4 large chicken breasts, skinned, boned, and cut into 16 squares each
1 tablespoon plain yogurt
¼ teaspoon salt
¼ teaspoon ground turmeric
½ teaspoon curry powder
⅛ teaspoon ground cardamom
1 teaspoon lemon juice
1 teaspoon vinegar
16 thin slices onion
8 small tomatoes, halved

Combine the breast squares with all the ingredients except the onion and tomatoes and allow to marinate for at least 30 minutes. Thread on skewers 2 squares of chicken, 1 slice of onion, 2 squares of chicken, ½ tomato. Repeat until all the ingredients are used. Broil slowly over hot coals or under the broiler, 6 inches from the heat source. (*Serves 6 to 8*)

ETHIOPIAN HOT CHICKEN

- **1 three-pound fryer, disjointed**
- **Juice of 1 lemon**
- **1 teaspoon salt**
- **6 medium-sized onions, chopped**
- **¼ cup (½ stick) butter**
- **2 tablespoons chili powder**
- **2 tablespoons tomato paste**
- **¼ cup red wine**
- **½ teaspoon ground ginger**
- **½ teaspoon freshly ground pepper**
- **6 hard-cooked eggs, shelled but left whole**

Cover the chicken with boiling water and add the lemon juice and salt. Cover and simmer for 10 minutes, then remove the chicken and drain, reserving broth. Brown the onions lightly in the butter, stirring constantly. Add 1 cup of the hot chicken broth, the chili powder, and tomato paste. Blend well and simmer together for 5 minutes, then add the wine, ginger, pepper, and another cup of hot broth.

Place the chicken in the sauce and simmer until the bird is tender (about 35 minutes). About 3 minutes before serving, prick the eggs all over with the tines of a fork to let the sauce permeate them. Add the eggs to the sauce and cook until just heated through. Serve with rice. (*Serves 4 to 6*)

FRENCH COQ AU VIN

- 1 three-pound chicken, disjointed
- All-purpose flour
- ¼ cup (½ stick) butter
- 2 ounces salt pork, diced and soaked in hot water
- 8 small white onions, peeled
- 4 green onions, white part only, minced
- 16 mushroom caps
- 1 clove garlic, put through a press
- ¼ cup brandy, warmed
- 1 teaspoon salt
- ½ teaspoon freshly ground pepper
- 1 sprig fresh parsley, minced
- 1½ cups red wine

Dredge the chicken parts in flour and brown lightly in the butter. Push to one side of the pan, then add the salt pork, white onions and green onions, mushrooms, and garlic. Cook only until very lightly browned, then remove vegetables with a slotted spoon and set aside. Add the brandy to the pan and flame (remember the long fireplace match!). When the flames die, add the salt, pepper, and parsley, then add the wine. Cover and simmer for about 25 minutes. Add the onion and mushroom mixture, cover, and cook another 15 minutes, or until the chicken is fork tender. (*Serves 4*)

GREEK CHICKEN WITH OKRA

- 3 pounds chicken parts
- Salt and freshly ground pepper to taste
- 3 pounds fresh okra
- ½ cup vinegar
- ¾ cup (1½ sticks) butter
- 1 onion, chopped
- 1½ pounds canned tomatoes, strained
- 2 cups water

Season the chicken parts with salt and pepper and set aside. Wash and carefully trim the okra, then arrange in a flat pan, pour the vinegar over, and set in the sun for 45 minutes.

Meanwhile, brown the butter in a deep saucepan or Dutch oven. Add the chicken and sauté until brown, then add the onion and let it brown. Add the tomatoes and boil for 4 to 5 minutes. Add the water, blend, and simmer for 30 minutes. Add the okra and simmer, covered, until tender. When the dish is almost finished, check it to make sure it isn't burning; the okra should absorb the liquid, leaving only the oil. (*Serves 6 to 8*)

HUNGARIAN CHICKEN PAPRIKASH

1 three-pound chicken, disjointed
Salt to taste
⅓ cup butter or lard
1 cup sliced onion
1 tablespoon good-quality imported paprika
2 cups boiling water
1 green pepper, cut into rings
1 cup sour cream

Sprinkle the chicken parts with salt and set aside. Melt the butter or lard in a Dutch oven and sauté the sliced onion in it until golden. Remove the onion and brown the chicken on both sides in the same fat, then replace the onion and sprinkle the paprika over both. Add the 2 cups boiling water and the pepper rings, then cover and simmer until the chicken is fork tender (about 30 minutes). Carefully add the sour cream, reheat without boiling, and serve at once with noodles. (*Serves 4*)

ITALIAN CHICKEN RISOTTO

1 cup raw long-grain rice
4 pounds chicken parts
3 tablespoons all-purpose flour
¼ cup vegetable oil
1 medium onion, chopped
1 clove garlic, put through a press
1 cup chopped celery
1 teaspoon salt
3 strands saffron, crushed
½ cup water
1 ten-and-one-half-ounce can condensed beef consommé
1 one-pound can cut green beans, drained
¼ cup toasted almonds
1 tablespoon minced fresh parsley

Spread the rice in a shallow baking pan and toast in a 350° oven, stirring occasionally, for 15 minutes, or until golden brown. Empty into a strainer, rinse under cold water, and set aside. Remove the skin from the chicken parts and discard. Shake the chicken in a paper bag with the flour until each piece is nicely coated, then brown in the oil in a large frying pan. Remove and reserve. In the same pan, sauté the onion and garlic. Stir in the rice, celery, salt, saffron, and water, then pour into a shallow baking dish. Arrange the chicken on top, then pour consommé over all, and cover.

Bake in a 350° oven for 1 hour and 20 minutes, or until the rice has absorbed all the liquid and is dry and fluffy. Spoon the beans over the chicken in little mounds, then cover and bake another 10 minutes. Sprinkle the top of the casserole with almonds and parsley and serve. (*Serves 6*)

JAPANESE YAKITORI

- ½ cup Japanese rice wine (sake) or sherry
- ½ cup soy sauce
- 1½ tablespoons granulated sugar
- 1 teaspoon freshly ground pepper
- 1 three-pound fryer, disjointed

Combine the wine, soy sauce, sugar, and pepper in a saucepan and simmer for 15 minutes. Place the chicken pieces in a deep bowl and pour the marinade over. Allow to stand overnight, turning the chicken once or twice. Cook the chicken over hot coals or under the broiler, 6 inches from the heat source, for 2 to 3 minutes, brushing liberally with marinade, then turn and brush again. Repeat until all the sauce is used and the chicken is nicely browned on all sides. The chicken is fully cooked when the juices run yellow. (*Serves 4 to 6*)

LIBERIAN CHICKEN-RICE HOT POT

- 1 three-and-one-half-pound chicken, disjointed
- 1 tablespoon salt
- 3 teaspoons pepper
- All-purpose flour
- ¼ cup (½ stick) butter
- ½ pound boiled ham, diced
- 3 quarts water, more if necessary
- 1 large onion, sliced
- ⅓ cup tomato paste
- ½ cup finely sliced cabbage
- 2½ cups raw brown rice

Season the chicken with the salt and pepper and allow to stand for about 15 minutes, then sprinkle with flour and brown lightly in bubbling hot butter. Remove from the skillet and place in a Dutch oven. Fry the diced ham in the remaining fat, then add to the chicken. Add the 3 quarts water to the Dutch oven, along with the onion, tomato paste, and cabbage. Cover and simmer for about 20 minutes, or until the chicken is tender.

Remove the chicken from the pot and add the rice. Cover and cook for 45 minutes, stirring occasionally. (It may be necessary to add a little boiling water during the cooking process, but don't let the rice become soggy.) Return the chicken to the rice, heat thoroughly, and serve. (*Serves 8*)

MEXICAN CHICKEN WITH BACON

3 teaspoons chili powder
3 cloves garlic, put through a press
4 slices bacon, cut ¼ inch thick
1 four- to five-pound roasting chicken, giblets reserved
2 large onions, sliced
1 green pepper, chopped
¼ cup (½ stick) butter
1 cup tomato paste
3 tablespoons minced fresh parsley
1½ tablespoons granulated sugar
1 teaspoon salt
½ cup sherry
2 teaspoons cornstarch

Combine one teaspoon of the chili powder with one clove of the garlic and spread the bacon slices with the mixture. Roll each slice up tightly, skewer with toothpicks, and place in the cavity of the chicken. Secure the cavity with small skewers or with thread, then place the chicken, breast side down, in a Dutch oven, along with the heart, liver and gizzard.

In a skillet, sauté the onions, remaining garlic, and green pepper in the butter until the vegetables are soft. Add the tomato paste, parsley, sugar, salt, remaining chili powder, and sherry, and when the mixture boils, pour it over the chicken and add enough boiling water to just cover three-quarters of the bird. Cover and cook at a simmer until the chicken is tender, turning the bird occasionally and adding enough water to keep the broth at its original level.

When the chicken is tender, remove it from the pot and take as much meat from the bones as possible; bits and pieces are all right, of course, but nice slices are preferable. Remove the bacon from the chicken cavity, cube and add to the chicken meat.

Put the bones into the pot and simmer for another 30 minutes. Strain the sauce and thicken slightly with the cornstarch mixed with a little cold water. Pour half the sauce over the chicken-bacon and pass the remainder in a sauceboat. (*Serves 6*)

MOLOKAI CHICKEN

5 tablespoons butter
2 cloves garlic, put through a press
6 green onions, green part and all, sliced thin
2 tablespoons all-purpose flour
1 teaspoon monosodium glutamate
1 cup dry white wine
1 cup sliced mushrooms
1 six-ounce can bamboo shoots, cubed
1 eight-ounce can water chestnuts, drained and sliced
2 cups pineapple chunks, drained
3 cups diced, cooked chicken
1 cup chopped macadamia nuts or cashews

Melt the butter in a large skillet and add the garlic and onions, cooking gently until soft. Blend the flour and monosodium glutamate and stir into the onion mixture, then add the wine and cook over low heat until the mixture boils gently and thickens. Add the mushrooms, bamboo shoots, and water chestnuts and simmer for 5 minutes. Stir in the pineapple chunks and diced chicken, cooking only long enough to heat them through. Sprinkle with the chopped nuts and serve with boiled or steamed rice. (*Serves 6 to 8*)

PAKISTANI STUFFED CHICKEN

Chicken

1 onion
1 small to medium-sized piece of fresh ginger
1 teaspoon salt
2 tablespoons freshly ground pepper
1 cup plain yogurt
1 four-pound roasting chicken
¼ cup (½ stick) butter

Stuffing

Juice of 1 lemon
4 small potatoes, boiled and diced
2 hard-cooked eggs, diced
2 tablespoons blanched, chopped almonds
¼ cup seedless raisins

Shred the onion and ginger together. Mix with the salt, pepper, and yogurt and spread over the entire chicken, then pierce the chicken all over with a kitchen fork and carefully rub the mixture in so the flavors will penetrate the meat. Let stand for 1 hour while you make the stuffing.

Sprinkle the lemon juice over the potatoes and eggs and

blend in the almonds and raisins. Stuff and truss the chicken.

Melt the butter in a Dutch oven, add the chicken, and cover. Cook very slowly for about 2 hours, or until fork tender, turning frequently. (*Serves 4 to 6*)

PHILIPPINE CHICKEN ADOBO

2 two-and-one-half- to three-pound chickens, disjointed
¾ cup water
¼ cup cider vinegar
1 tablespoon minced garlic
2 teaspoons salt
1 teaspoon freshly ground pepper
½ cup vegetable oil

Put the chicken parts into a Dutch oven and add the water, vinegar, garlic, salt, and pepper. Cover, bring to a boil, and cook over very low heat for about 40 minutes, or until tender, stirring from time to time. Drain off the liquid and discard, then remove chicken parts. Add the oil to the kettle, and when it is hot, sauté the chicken for about 7 minutes, or until lightly browned on all sides. (*Serves 6*)

PORTUGUESE STEWED CHICKEN

2 tablespoons flour
1 tablespoon salt
Few grindings of fresh pepper
1 three-pound fryer, disjointed
¼ cup olive oil
1 large onion, chopped
1 clove garlic, put through a press
3 tablespoons minced fresh parsley
3 tomatoes
1 teaspoon ground coriander seed

- 1 teaspoon seasoned salt
- 1 cup hot water
- ½ cup port wine
- 1 green pepper, cut in 1-inch cubes

Combine the flour, salt, and pepper in a paper bag and shake the chicken parts in the mixture until they are thoroughly coated. Heat the oil in a large skillet. Add the chicken and brown well on all sides, then remove the chicken and set aside. Sauté the onion and garlic in remaining oil until golden, then stir in 2 tablespoons of the parsley, 2 of the tomatoes, chopped, the coriander, and seasoned salt. Replace the chicken parts in the skillet and add the hot water and half the port wine.

Bring to a boil and simmer, covered, over low heat for 15 minutes, then add the green pepper and simmer another 15 minutes, or until the chicken is tender and the green pepper is cooked but still crisp. Pour in the remaining port wine, blend, and bring to a boil. Transfer to a heated platter and garnish with wedges of the remaining tomato and sprinkle with the remaining parsley. Serve hot, with noodles. (*Serves 4 to 6*)

PUERTO RICAN CHICKEN ASOPAO

- ¼ cup all-purpose flour
- 2 teaspoons salt
- ¼ teaspoon pepper
- 1 three-pound chicken, disjointed
- ¼ cup (½ stick) butter
- 3 cups chicken broth or stock, more if necessary
- 1 cup raw rice
- 1 four-ounce jar pimientos, drained and quartered
- 10 large stuffed green olives, sliced
- 1 ten-ounce package frozen cut asparagus
- ½ ten-ounce package frozen peas

Combine the flour, salt, and pepper and dredge the chicken pieces in the mixture. Sauté the chicken in hot butter until golden brown on both sides, then place in a Dutch oven and add the chicken broth or stock. Cover and simmer until the chicken is almost tender (about 25 minutes). Add the rice, pimientos, olives, asparagus, and peas and simmer for about 20 minutes, or until the rice and vegetables are cooked and tender, stirring a couple of times and adding a little more broth, if necessary. Serve in deep soup bowls. (*Serves 4 to 6*)

SPANISH CHICKEN-LOBSTER

½ cup olive oil
5 pounds chicken parts
⅓ cup minced shallots
5 cloves garlic, put through a press
½ cup finely chopped onion
4 tomatoes, peeled, seeded, and chopped
3 tablespoons tomato paste
½ cup blanched, toasted almonds
Salt and freshly ground pepper to taste
½ cup dry white wine, more if necessary
½ cup chicken broth, more if necessary
6 lobster tails, cut into chunks
3 tablespoons minced fresh parsley

Heat half the oil in a Dutch oven and lightly brown the chicken parts, then remove the chicken and set aside. Add another 2 tablespoons oil to the Dutch oven and cook the shallots, garlic, and onion for 4 minutes, without browning. Add the tomatoes, tomato paste, and almonds, season with salt and pepper, and simmer for 5 minutes. Replace the chicken parts in the pot and add the wine and chicken broth. Cover and simmer for about 30 minutes.

Meanwhile, in another pan, sauté the lobster chunks

in the remaining olive oil for about 2 minutes, then add to the chicken in the pot and baste with the sauce. Cover and simmer another 30 minutes. (If the sauce reduces too much, add equal amounts of wine and chicken broth.) Garnish with parsley and serve hot. *(Serves 8)*

TASMANIAN FRUITED CHICKEN

1 three-pound chicken, disjointed
Salt and freshly ground pepper to taste
6 tablespoons butter
1 large onion, cut into eighths
1 green pepper, cut into strips
1 twenty-nine-ounce can sliced peaches
¼ cup red wine vinegar
2 tablespoons soy sauce
1 tablespoon cornstarch
1 four-and-one-half-ounce jar whole button mushrooms

Season the chicken with salt and pepper and brown on both sides in the butter. Cover and cook until tender (about 30 to 40 minutes), then remove to a warm platter. Add the onion and green pepper and cook until tender, without browning.

Drain the peaches, mixing 1 cup of the syrup with the vinegar, soy sauce, and cornstarch. Add the syrup mixture to the vegetables and cook and stir until thickened. Add the peaches, mushrooms, and the cooked chicken and heat thoroughly. (*Serves 6*)

21 Leftovers

Odds, Ends, and Afterthoughts

Self-explanatory: a veritable grab-bag of fowl fare.

CHICKEN CROQUETTES I

1 tablespoon butter
1 tablespoon all-purpose flour
½ cup milk
1 cup finely chopped, cooked chicken
⅓ cup finely chopped mushrooms
½ teaspoon salt
2 tablespoons prepared mustard
1 whole egg
1 tablespoon cold water
Cracker crumbs
Shortening for frying

Melt the butter in a saucepan and stir in the flour. Add the milk gradually and cook, stirring constantly, until the sauce is thick and bubbly. Add the chicken and mushrooms to the sauce, along with the salt and mustard, and mix thoroughly. Chill for about 30 minutes, and when the mixture has chilled enough to be workable, shape it into 4 patties. Chill again for about 2 hours.

Beat the egg lightly and mix it with the water. Coat the

chilled patties with cracker crumbs, dip in the egg mixture, and coat again with crumbs. Fry in hot shortening until brown on all sides and serve immediately. (*Serves 4*)

CHICKEN CROQUETTES II

2 tablespoons vegetable oil
2 teaspoons minced onion
¼ cup all-purpose flour
1 teaspoon salt
Freshly ground pepper to taste
1 cup milk
2 cups minced, cooked chicken
1 teaspoon minced fresh parsley
Bread crumbs
1 egg, beaten with 2 tablespoons water
Fat for deep frying

Heat the oil, then add the onion and fry until golden. Blend in the flour, salt, and pepper. Add the milk gradually and cook, stirring constantly, until the mixture thickens. Add the chicken and parsley and mix well. Chill thoroughly.

Form the chilled mixture into croquettes. Roll in crumbs, dip in the egg-water mixture, and roll again in crumbs. Fry in deep fat at 370° until golden brown, then drain on paper toweling. Serve very hot. (*Serves 6*)

CHICKEN CROQUETTES III

- 2 cups minced, cooked chicken
- ½ cup flaked coconut
- Salt, freshly ground pepper, and curry powder to taste
- Pinch of ground mace
- 1 cup hot béchamel sauce (medium white sauce made with 2 tablespoons butter, 2 tablespoons all-purpose flour, and 1 cup blended chicken broth and cream instead of milk)
- 1 whole egg
- 2 tablespoons brandy
- ⅓ cup dry bread crumbs
- ⅓ cup chopped, blanched almonds or cashews
- Vegetable oil for deep frying

Combine the chicken, coconut, and seasonings, then blend in the béchamel sauce. Spread on a platter and chill. When chilled, shape into 8 croquettes.

Beat the egg lightly, then slowly and carefully stir in the brandy. Dip the croquettes in the egg-brandy mixture and roll in the combined crumbs and nuts. Brown in deep oil (370°), then drain on paper toweling. Serve with a curry sauce and coconut-topped rice. (*Serves 8*)

CHICKEN HASH I

- 4 green onions or shallots, minced
- 3 tablespoons chicken fat
- 2 cups minced, cooked chicken
- 1 cup half-and-half
- ½ teaspoon dried tarragon
- Salt to taste
- 4 slices toast
- 4 poached eggs

Combine all the ingredients except the toast and eggs and heat well in a skillet. Serve on the toast, each portion topped with an egg. (*Serves 4*)

CHICKEN HASH II

1½ cups cooked chicken
3 raw potatoes
1 onion
1 green pepper
2 tablespoons butter
½ cup canned, drained tomatoes
½ cup chicken stock
Salt and freshly ground pepper to taste

Chop together the chicken, potatoes, onion, and green pepper, then brown in the butter. Add tomatoes, stock, salt, and pepper and cook gently for about 30 minutes. (*Serves 6*)

CHICKEN HASH III

2 tablespoons butter
2 tablespoons all-purpose flour
2 cups chicken broth
2 cups chopped, cooked chicken
2 cups chopped, cooked potatoes
1 teaspoon grated onion
Salt to taste
Freshly ground pepper to taste
4 to 6 slices cold boiled ham
Chopped fresh parsley for garnish

Melt the butter, then add the flour and blend well. Add the chicken broth and cook until thick, stirring constantly. Add the chicken, potatoes, and onion, season to taste with salt and pepper, and heat thoroughly. Brown the ham slices lightly and serve the hash on top, garnished with chopped parsley. (*Serves 4 to 6*)

HOT CHICKEN LOAF

- **¼ pound mushrooms, sliced thin**
- **1 tablespoon butter**
- **1 cup soft bread crumbs**
- **1 cup milk**
- **1 cup well-seasoned chicken broth**
- **2 eggs, beaten well**
- **½ teaspoon salt**
- **¼ teaspoon paprika**
- **¼ cup finely sliced pimiento**
- **3 cups finely cut-up, cooked chicken**

Sauté the mushrooms gently in the butter for 20 minutes. Combine the bread crumbs with the milk and broth, then add the eggs, salt, paprika, pimiento, chicken, and sautéed mushrooms. Mix well. Pour into a well-greased loaf pan, set in a larger pan containing hot water, and bake in a 350° oven for 1 hour, or until the loaf is firm.

Turn the loaf onto a hot platter and serve with a mushroom sauce. (*Serves 6 to 8*)

COLD CHICKEN LOAF

- **3 cups finely chopped, cooked chicken**
- **2 cups sour cream**
- **2 cups soft bread crumbs**

2 eggs, beaten
1 tablespoon chopped onion
2 stalks celery, chopped
1 teaspoon salt
¼ teaspoon dried marjoram
Sliced, stuffed olives for garnish (optional)

Combine all the ingredients except the garnish, taste for seasoning, and pour into a greased loaf pan. Set the pan in another one containing hot water and bake in a 350° oven for about 1 hour, or until the loaf is firm. Remove from the oven and cool. Chill in the refrigerator. Turn onto a platter and garnish with overlapping slices of stuffed olives, or serve presliced. (*Serves 6 to 8*)

CHICKEN SHORTCAKE

5 tablespoons all-purpose flour
2½ cups chicken broth
2 four-ounce cans button mushrooms, drained but liquid reserved
4 small potatoes, peeled and cubed
8 very small white onions
1 cup fresh or frozen peas
5 to 6 cups diced, cooked chicken
½ cup chopped pimiento
8 large baking powder biscuits, split

Blend the flour with ½ cup of the broth in a saucepan. Gradually stir in the remaining broth and the reserved mushroom liquid. Bring to a boil, stirring constantly, then add the potatoes and onions. Simmer for 15 minutes, then add the peas and simmer until all the vegetables are tender. Stir in the chicken, mushrooms, and pimiento and cook just long enough to heat through. Serve over the split biscuits. (*Serves 8*)

CHICKEN SCRAPPLE

- **1½ teaspoons salt**
- **3½ cups chicken broth**
- **1½ cups yellow cornmeal**
- **½ cup cold water**
- **¼ teaspoon pepper**
- **¼ to ½ teaspoon curry powder**
- **2 cups cooked chicken, put through the coarse blade of a food grinder**
- **3 tablespoons butter**
- **All-purpose flour**
- **Hot tomato sauce**

Add the salt to the chicken broth and bring to a rapid boil. Combine the cornmeal, water, and seasonings and mix thoroughly. Add to the broth, stirring constantly, and cook about 15 minutes. Stir in the chicken and turn into a greased loaf pan (7 x 2 x 9 inches). Chill thoroughly.

Melt the butter in a shallow baking pan. Unmold the chilled loaf and cut into 8 or 10 slices. Roll the slices in flour and arrange in the prepared baking pan. Bake at 400° for 20 to 25 minutes, or until lightly browned, then turn to brown the other side. Serve with hot tomato sauce. (*Serves 8 to 10*)

Note: If you prefer, the slices may be fried instead of baked.

CHICKEN PANCAKES I

Chicken filling

2 tablespoons butter
2 cups diced, cooked chicken
Pinch of cayenne pepper
½ teaspoon salt
Freshly ground pepper to taste
1 cup heavy cream

Pancakes

6 pancakes (about 6 inches in diameter)

Sauce

3 egg yolks
2 teaspoons lemon juice
Pinch of cayenne
½ cup (1 stick) butter
½ cup heavy cream, whipped

Prepare the chicken filling first. Melt half the butter and stir in the chicken and seasonings. Heat thoroughly, then stir in the cream and remaining butter. Cook and stir until the butter melts. Place the chicken mixture in the center of each pancake and roll up, jelly-roll fashion. Arrange side by side in a greased shallow baking dish and keep warm while you prepare the sauce.

Put the egg yolks, lemon juice, and cayenne in a blender container and whir to blend quickly. Melt the butter until sizzling, then turn the blender on high and pour the hot butter into the eggs in a thin stream until well blended and thick. Fold in the whipped cream lightly. Top the pancakes with the sauce. (*Serves 6*)

CHICKEN PANCAKES II

¼ cup (½ stick) butter
2 tablespoons all-purpose flour
1 cup chicken broth
1 egg yolk, beaten
½ cup half-and-half
1 tablespoon chopped onion
¼ cup chopped mushrooms
2 tablespoons minced, cooked ham
2 cups chopped, cooked chicken
2 teaspoons sherry
6 thin pancakes
6 mushroom caps, cooked in butter

Melt 2 tablespoons of the butter in a saucepan and stir in the flour. Add the chicken broth and cook, stirring, until thickened and smooth. Combine the egg yolk and half-and-half and gradually stir into the sauce. Pour ½ cup of the sauce into a shallow baking dish and set aside.

Brown the onion, chopped mushrooms, ham, and chicken in the remaining butter. Add 2 tablespoons of the sauce, plus the sherry, and mix well. Spread some of the mixture on each pancake and roll up. Place the pancakes on top of the sauce in the baking dish and top each with a mushroom cap. Brush with butter. Heat in a 375° oven for 10 to 15 minutes and serve with the remaining sauce. (*Serves 6*)

CHICKEN FRITTERS

2 whole chicken breasts, cooked, boned, skinned, and cut into 8 pieces
1 cup packaged pancake mix

2/3 cup milk
1/2 teaspoon salt
1/4 teaspoon freshly ground pepper
Fat for frying

Dip the chicken "bites" into a batter made of the pancake mix, milk, salt, and pepper. Fry them in about 1/2 inch of hot fat in a skillet, then drain on paper toweling. Serve very hot, with maple syrup. (*Serves 4*)

CHICKEN TIMBALES

1/2 cup soft bread crumbs
2/3 cup milk
2 tablespoons butter
1/2 teaspoon salt
1/8 teaspoon paprika
Freshly ground pepper to taste
2 teaspoons minced fresh parsley
2 whole eggs
1 cup finely chopped, cooked chicken or 1/2 cup each finely chopped, cooked chicken and chicken livers
Chicken gravy (see, for example, page 171) with minced parsley

Cook the bread crumbs in the milk for about 10 minutes, or until thickish. Add the butter, salt, paprika, pepper, and parsley. Beat the eggs until light and combine with the chicken. Lightly fold the egg-chicken mixture into the bread crumb–milk mixture, then fill well-greased custard molds two-thirds full.

Set the molds on a rack in a pan that can hold hot water to half the depth of the timbale mixture. Cover each mold with a round of foil or waxed paper to keep the tops soft and bake in a 325° oven for about 20 minutes, or until a knife inserted in the center of a timbale comes out clean. Unmold and serve at once with hot chicken gravy. (*Serves 4 to 6*)

CHICKEN SOUFFLÉ

6 medium potatoes
2 eggs, separated
2 teaspoons salt
¼ teaspoon white pepper
2 cups diced, cooked chicken
¼ cup blanched, slivered almonds

Peel the potatoes and cook in salted water just until done, then drain thoroughly and mash with an electric beater until very light and fluffy. Add the egg yolks, salt, and pepper and beat until smooth. Add the chicken and blend well. Beat the egg whites until very stiff and carefully and gently fold them into the potato mixture.

Pile the mixture lightly in a buttered casserole and bake at 350° for about 15 to 20 minutes, or until the top is golden. Sprinkle with the almonds just before serving. (*Serves 6*)

CHICKEN PATTIES WITH GRAVY

1 cup minced, cooked chicken
1 egg, lightly beaten
¼ cup fine, dry bread crumbs
¼ cup minced onion
1 tablespoon minced fresh parsley
1 cup chicken gravy (see page 171)
2 tablespoons butter

Combine all the ingredients except ⅔ cup of the gravy and the butter. Form into 4 patties and brown in the butter. Serve with the remaining gravy. (*Serves 4*)

CHICKEN CAKES WITH SWEET POTATOES

2½ cups ground cooked chicken breasts
5 medium sweet potatoes, cooked and mashed
⅓ cup minced green onions
1 egg yolk
¼ cup all-purpose flour
Salt and freshly ground pepper to taste
3 tablespoons white wine
¼ cup vegetable oil
1 ten-and-one-half-ounce can cream of mushroom soup, undiluted

Combine all the ingredients except the oil and soup. Form into a round ball like dough and work it until well blended, then chill about 2 hours.

When ready to cook, form the mixture into 2-inch patties and fry in the oil in a heavy skillet. Cook until browned and slightly crusted on both sides. Serve with the mushroom soup, heated, as the sauce. (*Serves 6 to 8*)

HOT CHICKEN ROLLS

1 ten-and-one-half-ounce can cream of mushroom soup, undiluted
⅓ cup chicken broth
½ teaspoon Worcestershire sauce
Pinch of poultry seasoning
1 cup diced, cooked chicken
4 sesame-topped hamburger buns or other soft rolls
Butter
1 egg, hard-cooked and chopped
2 to 3 tablespoons toasted sesame seeds

In the top of a double boiler, over boiling water, heat the soup, broth, Worcestershire, poultry seasoning, and chicken. Split and butter, then toast the buns in the broiler and set the bottom sections on 4 plates. Pour half the chicken mixture over them. Top with the seeded bun halves and the remainder of the chicken. Sprinkle with chopped egg and toasted sesame seeds and serve at once. (*Serves 4*)

SOUTHERN CHICKEN ROLL

1¼ cups diced, cooked chicken
⅓ cup chopped ripe olives
1 teaspoon minced onion
1 tablespoon chopped pimiento
⅛ teaspoon paprika
1 recipe packaged baking powder biscuits
⅓ cup shortening
Chicken gravy (see page 171)
Pimiento strips for garnish

Combine the chicken, olives, onion, pimiento, and paprika. Prepare the biscuit dough, adding the ⅓ cup shortening. Roll out to a thickness of ¼ inch and spread with the chicken mixture. Roll up like a jelly roll and place, seam side down, in a greased, shallow pan. Bake in a 425° oven for 15 to 20 minutes, then remove to a hot platter, cover with gravy, and garnish with pimiento strips. (*Serves 6*)

HOT CHICKEN-HAM SANDWICH

4 slices spiced ham
4 slices cooked chicken (or equivalent in cooked pieces)
4 pieces unbuttered toast
Leftover chicken gravy (see page 171)
1 cup sliced, sautéed mushrooms
Grated Swiss cheese

Stack the ham and chicken on the toast, then top with the gravy and mushrooms. Sprinkle generously with cheese and brown under the broiler until the cheese melts. (*Serves 4*)

VIRGINIA CHICKEN SANDWICH

1½ cups diced, cooked chicken
¼ cup crumbled blue cheese
½ cup chopped celery
3 tablespoons mayonnaise
8 slices buttered bread

Combine the chicken, cheese, celery, and mayonnaise and spread generously on 4 slices of the bread. Top with the remaining slices and cut in quarters. (*Serves 4*)

CURRIED CHICKEN SANDWICHES

- **½ cup sour cream**
- **1 tablespoon honey**
- **1 teaspoon salt**
- **1 teaspoon prepared mustard**
- **¼ teaspoon curry powder**
- **12 thin slices white bread, crusts removed**
- **Softened butter**
- **1½ cups minced, cooked chicken**
- **½ cup chopped walnuts**

Combine the sour cream, honey, salt, mustard, and curry powder and mix well, then allow to stand about 30 minutes for the flavors to meld. Meanwhile, spread the bread with butter. Stir the chicken and nuts into the sour cream mixture, then spread on half the bread slices. Top with the remaining slices and refrigerate for about 15 minutes. Cut into quarters and serve. (*Serves 6*)

CHICKEN BASKETS

Baskets

- **5 cups fresh breadcrumbs**
- **⅓ cup minced onion**
- **Salt and freshly ground pepper to taste**
- **½ cup melted butter**

Filling

- **2 cups diced, cooked chicken**
- **½ cup chopped celery**
- **⅓ cup chopped green pepper**

2 tablespoons chopped pimiento
3 tablespoons chopped onion
2 tablespoons lemon juice
1 teaspoon salt
½ cup mayonnaise
⅓ cup grated sharp Cheddar cheese

To make the baskets, combine all the basket ingredients, tossing lightly with the butter. Divide the mixture between six buttered custard cups or ramekins (5-ounce size). Press the mixture firmly over the bottoms and sides, then bake 20 minutes in a 375° oven. Cool.

Combine all the ingredients for the filling except the cheese and blend well. Place about ½ cup of the mixture in each of the crumb baskets in the custard cups. Top each with grated cheese, then bake 20 minutes in a 375° oven.

The baskets may be served hot, right from the custard cups, or may be chilled for a nice summer luncheon dish. If you opt for the latter, allow the cups to cool thoroughly before setting in the refrigerator to chill. Just before serving, very carefully unmold the crumb baskets. (*Serves 6*)

Note: These are especially good accompanied by a small fresh fruit salad.

CHICKEN GRATINÉE

3 cups cooked rice
1 three-pound chicken, cooked, skinned, boned, and cut into nice-sized pieces
1 cup rich chicken stock
¼ cup heavy cream
3 egg yolks
¼ cup grated Swiss cheese
2 tablespoons butter

Make a bed of the rice in the bottom of a greased, fairly shallow oven-to-table dish. Arrange the chicken over the rice, then beat the stock into a mixture of the cream, egg yolks, and cheese. Pour the sauce over the chicken, dot with the butter, and broil until golden brown. (*Serves 6*)

CHICKEN PILAF I

1 three-pound fryer, disjointed
½ cup (1 stick) butter
½ cup chopped onion
1 green pepper, chopped
1 tablespoon ground turmeric
1 teaspoon ground ginger
1 teaspoon ground cinnamon
1 teaspoon salt
¼ teaspoon freshly ground pepper
⅛ teaspoon crushed hot peppers
3½ cups tomato purée
2 cups cooked rice

Brown the chicken pieces on both sides in the butter, along with the chopped onion. Add all the other ingredients except the rice and stir to blend, then cover and simmer gently until the chicken is very tender.

Remove the chicken to a hot plate and stir the cooked rice into the sauce. When the rice is thoroughly heated, transfer to a shallow baking dish and place the chicken on top. Bake in a 350° oven until good and hot. Serve with chutney. (*Serves 4*)

CHICKEN PILAF II

1 three-and-one-half-pound stewing chicken
1 quart water
3 teaspoons salt
Pinch of freshly ground pepper
1 bay leaf
1 onion, chopped
1½ cups raw rice
2 eggs, hard-cooked and chopped
⅛ teaspoon dried red peppers, crushed

Cut the chicken into serving pieces and place in a large pot or Dutch oven with the water, 1 teaspoon of the salt, the pepper, bay leaf, and onion. Cover and simmer 1½ hours, or until the chicken is tender. Remove the chicken, and when it has cooled, skin it and cut the meat from the bones in largish pieces. Remove the bay leaf.

Cook the stock rapidly, uncovered, until it has reduced to about 3 cups. Add the rice and remaining salt, then cover and simmer over very low heat until the stock is almost absorbed. Add the chicken, egg, and red peppers, then cover and steam for 5 minutes. (*Serves 6 to 8*)

Afterword

This compendium of chicken cookery might have swelled to encyclopedic size had its publisher, Harper & Row, not put down its authoritative foot at perhaps just the right moment. But my files still grow. As a notorious "chicken hawk" from way back, I have become the recipient of just about every feathered recipe that has tickled the fancy of family, friends, and dozens of loyal fans.

And speaking of them—it is always something of a shock to me to realize that most of my "new" fans were born much too late ever to have seen me on the screen—or even on the late, late show. Thank God, I say, for this new cult of cinematic nostalgia burgeoning among the young! It keeps *me* young, too, to be loved and remembered.

Bless you all. To all of you—family and friends—I tardily dedicate the "goodness" inherent in this book.

J. N.

Index

74 75 76 77 78 10 9 8 7 6 5 4 3 2 1